Still Ha√

A Husband's Story About a 21-Year War with Breast Cancer

By Michael D. Stalter

1

Still Have Faith

*A Husband's Story About a 21 Year War
with Breast Cancer*

By Michael D. Stalter

Edited by Elizabeth Reynolds, PhD

Proofread by Arlene Elberson

Author Photo Back cover "Sweet memories"; Photography: Sandy Whisker

Publication Data

ISBN Number 978-1-60458-823-1

Copyright 1-660077931_Application_20110913_110439

This book is dedicated to all of the people who have touched my life and who will touch my life. They made me who I am today and who I will be tomorrow.

One dollar from every book sold will be donated to cancer research.

I asked for Strength, and God gave me Struggles to make me Strong.

I asked for Wisdom, and God gave me Challenges to Resolve.

I asked for Courage, and God gave me Fear to Overcome.

I asked for Blessings, and God Blessed me.

"There is no worse death than the end of hope." Clive Owen, King Arthur, the film.

This is a story about a husband's emotions, feelings, and struggles in dealing with his wife's 17½ year battle with breast cancer and the 4 years since her death. Over this time period Mike had to deal with the deaths of other family members, raising his two children, his relationship with God, and rebuilding his life. It is a very compelling story written from a man's perspective on how men think and feel in a very down-to-Earth style like it is being told to the reader by a friend.

For every book sold $1 will be donated to cancer research.

Contents

INTRODUCTION

It was Saturday, September 22, 1990. It was a day that I had been dreading for months, my 30th birthday. I'd been lying awake at nights all that summer thinking about being 30, scared about being 30. I wouldn't be in my teens or my 20s anymore, but someone who was getting older in their 30s. Thirty really bothered me. I just couldn't get it out of my mind. And now it was here, and I didn't want to wake up that day. I was feeling weird, realizing the sun was coming in around the window shades. My eyes were still closed, but I could sort of sense and feel the light. I was trying to shut the brightness out of this shitty day. I just kept thinking I wanted to go back to sleep, I didn't want to be 30.

I couldn't shake that fuzzy feeling that a person has when they first wake up but yet aren't awake. All I knew was I didn't want to be 30. However, in those first few seconds that I was waking up and thinking all this, I started realizing someone was up next to me, rubbing, hugging, kissing me, and it felt pretty fantastic. That someone was my wife, Mary, who didn't do that very often. She normally let me start things. So this was a nice change. When Mary saw me waking up, she smiled real big. She had big brown eyes, and

I thought she was beautiful, and she said, "Happy Birthday!" So I guess turning 30 had some benefits.

Looking back these 21 years to that moment, I remember everything. It was the last time we truly made love before her left breast was removed. It was the last time we made love without worrying if it would be the last time that we made love, and it would be the last time we made love without a big, black cloud hanging over our heads. I still remember how Mary looked. To me, she was perfect. Her waist, her breasts, the whole body, you know. At least it was perfect to me. And I'm sure if some Miss America judge would have looked at Mary, they would've found fault somewhere, but I couldn't. I loved her and she was the mother of my child, the woman who loved me, my best friend.

Between my birthday and the discovery of the lump in Mary's left breast on October 1, we had a couple of quickies that married people do with an 18-month old son, but on my birthday, that was the last time that my mind was truly free to just relax and be with Mary. That last time has stayed with me in my mind these two plus decades. Never again would I be able to look at her and marvel at how beautiful and perfect she was. She wouldn't have agreed with me, but there was something unspoiled and unquestionably picturesque about a woman's body when a man loves her and knows that woman loves him.

I didn't see the extra weight that Mary never lost after the birth of our son. I never saw the few scars she got growing up on the farm. I never saw anything but the perfect giving that we expect in the fairytale marriages that few people ever get to experience, and I was experiencing it. Other than I was turning 30 that day, my life was a fairytale up until then.

This is my story, a story about a husband's war with breast cancer. And when I say war, that's what I mean. It was and still is a war of survival, of existence, of gut-wrenching pain and agony that most people will never understand and never experience. In some ways, the war never ends, even almost four years since Mary's death from breast cancer. My story isn't about how great I was or am because I could've done so much more, nor is this a story about how romantic a terminal illness is, if we believe what Hollywood movies say.

Hopefully, my story will help some other men whose wives or significant others are battling breast cancer, because I'll talk about my feelings and my weaknesses along with the dogged desire to keep getting up after getting knocked down and not giving up hope. Sort of like in that Rocky Balboa movie when he's talking to his son and he says, "It's not how hard you can hit but how hard you can get hit by life and still keep going forward." And it's not a hope that cancer will go away magically, but my hope is that of rebuilding my life and the lives of my children now that Mary's gone, and to do what's right by my children, Tom and Sarah. It's a hope I have that God will bless me with a loving wife, a giving partner, and a best friend to share life with. Somebody to kick my ass and motivate me when I need it. Someone to comfort me in bad times, and someone to hold me when I feel alone.

When my war with breast cancer started, I had my father. His parents, my grandparents, my Grandpa and Grandma Stalter, along with a healthy mom. I don't have any of that now. My Grandpa Stalter died before Mary was even done with her first round of chemo, and my Grandma Stalter died three months after Grandpa and eight months after Mary was diagnosed, right after she was done with her first round of chemo. My Grandpa and Grandma Stalter were like a second set of parents to me, and to me, their love and support for the first 30 years of my life is something that I think about every day, and I draw strength from their memory.

My dad died four and a half months before Mary of a heart attack. He collapsed in front of me. In fact, he bounced down some stairs in front of me, and I had to pick him up and perform CPR on him until the ambulance came. My mom is just not healthy, and so all the people I started this war with now are gone.

My story is one of loss, losing the ones that helped give me strength to fight this worst fight of my life. And I've had a lot of fights. I grew up an only child, and maybe that made me a little different. Maybe that singled me out to possibly be picked on a little bit. But from grade school all through college, I seemed to get into fights. I wrestled in high school and college a little bit. I tried boxing a little bit in college, and then I started taking Tae Kwon Do in 1987. So I've been fighting and sparring with people just about my whole life. I've won more than I've lost, but that's not important. What is important is that I never gave up, no matter how many times I got knocked down, I never gave up. I always got back up.

From taking Tae Kwon Do for over 24 years, I never thought about not picking up a challenge, not sparring with somebody. And then my dad died, and I didn't want to get back up. Why was God doing this to me? What did He expect of me? Why did He keep giving me challenges? I felt so broken when Dad died, I felt no desire to keep on fighting. Even my children didn't seem to motivate me. I had truly given up. Whatever would happen to me would just happen. When Mary saw these things change in me, it scared her. She stopped trying to distance herself from me, which she thought would ease the pain of her death when she died. Mary got closer to me again and kicked me into gear. She motivated me to keep going and to keep fighting for our children, because they had no one else. I was really all Tom and Sarah had left.

Everyone that was close when this war started is gone. This war with breast cancer has taken a toll on me that I can't explain. But when new friends hear about my story, they seem amazed. Even my old friends seem to be amazed that I can keep on going and talk about what I went through. And they all tell me that I should share this story—my battle with breast cancer, my war with breast cancer, my fight with breast cancer, so that other men facing this can realize that there are others fighting the same fight and maybe not give up and maybe ask for help.

My friends are surprised that I'm not mad at God and that I haven't given up hope of finding the fairytale life I once had. I did and do still believe in fairytales, and even though fairytales have monsters that we have to conquer and get by, I still believe in them. And as I

12

write this introduction, I do see hope on the horizon, a flicker of hope at the end of a tunnel. I had a date on May 14, 2011, 28 years to the day that I had my first date with Mary. When I started writing this book I didn't know if this was just a date or the start of a fairytale, but as I finish writing this book I realize it wasn't just a date, nor was it the start of a fairytale. It was a wink from God to never give up hope because every date I have until I find my fairytale has to start with that first flicker of hope. My hope won't let me give up on life.

CHAPTER ONE

I Have a Lump.

For the most part, Mary and I lived a pretty idyllic life. We lived at 402 Chestnut Street which was on the corner of Chestnut and Walnut. It was a tree-lined brick street that was just pretty typical of an idyllic Midwestern small town. The bungalow was white, and it had a country style, as well as a country flavor for the interior. You'd walk in the back door and you could go upstairs to the kitchen, or you could go downstairs to the basement. The basement was unfinished, and that's where our laundry room was, and that's where we had the two dogs, Isis and Asta, both Rottweilers, with a fenced-in back yard.

When you walked up to the kitchen, it was a smaller kitchen. It really wasn't an eat-in kitchen, but it was pretty nice. And then you'd walk into the dining room which was wallpapered. Mary and her mom had put up a country-style wallpaper with a border about chair rail height, and from the dining room you could walk on into the living room which was painted sort of an off-white. We had a couch and a loveseat, a couple of end tables, a coffee table and a TV entertainment center. From the living room, you could go onto the enclosed front porch which covered the whole front of the house, or you could walk into the room that we used as the den/sewing room. Mary liked to sew as a hobby.

From there if you walked off the dining room, you'd walk into a little hallway, and from the hallway you could turn right to go to Tom's bedroom and left to go to our bedroom, or you could keep going straight to the bathroom. It was pretty typical... nothing really special, other than it was special to me. It was the place where we had conceived our son, Tom. When he was 18 months old, on October 1, 1990, Mary came home, walked in that back door, up those stairs, through the kitchen and into the dining room to see that my mom and dad were there. They were returning Tom. My mom had watched Tom that day, as she had done basically every day from the time he was six weeks old when Mary had gone back to work.

Mary had a really funny look on her face. I wasn't sure what was going on. I thought, "Well, is she upset because my parents are there?"

But yet she saw them quite a bit, since we dropped Tom off every morning. Was it work? I wasn't really sure. We both worked at the Pontiac Correctional Center which is a maximum security prison. To give you an idea of what the facility is like, watch the *Shawshank Redemption*. Pontiac is an old prison. I believe it is still the eighth oldest maximum security prison in the country. Mary worked in the Record Office as a file clerk, and I was the Business Manager, the assistant to the Chief Fiscal Officer. I guess if I had a fancy title, it would've been Assistant Chief Fiscal Officer.

Our work was fairly stressful, Mary's much more so, since she had to work under deadlines and legal ramifications if inmates didn't serve the right amount of time or if the right paperwork wasn't with inmates when they transferred from one prison to another.

So I wasn't sure why she was looking so funny when she walked in the house. I asked her how her physical went, and she said, "Okay."

It wasn't too much longer until mom and dad left, and then she just sort of looked funny. I asked her if she was mad, and she said no, that the doctor had found a lump.

We got to this point of having physicals a few weeks before, as I was turning 30.

I figured, "Well, it's time to get my physical." I'd gotten a physical about every other year since I had gotten out of college. When I was out for sports in high school and college and got a physical every year, and since college, I still jogged and tried to lift weights a little bit, but I pretty much still did the jogging and the running, along with the Tae Kwon Do. And so, I had lined up a physical for myself.

I told Mary and she said, "You know, I think maybe I should get one. I haven't had a physical since Tom was born."

She tried to get one with a gynecologist, but there was a six-month waiting list. Thank God she didn't wait. She got one with our family doctor, Dr. Hough, who was a fantastic doctor and still is a fantastic doctor. He found a lump on Mary's left breast. If you would draw a clock around her nipple, the lump was right around where the two would have been, just a little bit past the areola. She had me feel it. It felt like a lump. I wasn't sure what it was. She told me that Dr. Hough thought it was probably a blocked milk gland, but he wanted to be safe, and so he was going to schedule her for a mammogram probably later that week.

We put Tom to bed, did a few things around the house and then crawled into bed ourselves. We talked about the lump and what it could be. I tried to reassure her that it was probably just a blocked milk gland like Dr. Hough said, because he was really pretty sharp. I kept feeling the lump. It made me nervous, but I tried to make a joke out of it and act like I had fun comparing one breast to the other. There was a lump here but no lump there. So I played with her

17

breasts. I tried to get frisky, and I think Mary was going to let me. The problem was my penis wasn't cooperating. I couldn't get hard, I was too nervous. Somehow deep inside I was scared, scared like I hadn't been scared before, scared worse than when I had to walk down a cell house gallery when the inmates were running loose.

Several years before, when I was in college, I was dating another girl. She was upset because her mom had died from breast cancer. As we were talking about it, I could tell she was really scared and upset, I told her I would pray about it later. So after I dropped her off and I was driving home, I prayed that she wouldn't get cancer like she was worried about. Somehow a weird little voice in my head told me that that girl wouldn't get cancer but that I would marry somebody who would get breast cancer, and she would die from it. So, deep down inside, there was a pit in my stomach, a gnawing fear that I couldn't put away. As much as I wanted to be brave and tough and goofy so Mary wouldn't worry, I couldn't get hard. It seems to be a problem whenever I get nervous. My penis doesn't want to work. Oh, well, I guess that's life.

So later that week, Mary got a call that she had to go to the hospital on Friday, October 5, 1990, and get a mammogram. The mammogram was in the morning, and Mary took off work. For some

18

reason I took off work that day, as well, and I had Tom. I can't really remember why, but I had Tom with me. And so Mary went in the morning, and I was with Tom. When I got home, there was a call from the doctor's office on the answering machine, so I called them back. They wanted Mary to return to the hospital; to do a needle biopsy. We got this call a little before noon, and Mary wasn't home yet.

Luckily, she came home fairly soon and I told her, "Hey, they want you back up there for a needle biopsy," and she wasn't sure what that meant.

Well, I thought I did. Which at times seems to be a fault of mine, jumping to conclusions. When I was a kid, my mom had had mastitis, and every so often, she would have to go to the doctor's. They'd stick a needle in a lump and they'd drain the water off. So I was sure that's what it was. All of a sudden, relief flooded Mary's face. It flooded my insides. Wow, I'd dodged a bullet.

So we went to the hospital after we dropped Tom off at my mom and dad's. Mom was going to watch Tom. As we went bip-bopping into the Emergency Room, Dr. Hough was on call working in there for some reason, and they told us the bad news. They didn't like the shape of the lump.

"It looked like a gumball", as Dr. Hough described it, "when it starts getting the little lumps on it".

He said, "We're afraid it's cancer, and it's getting ready to shoot the tentacles out."

I was devastated. Mary was in shock. So they prepped Mary, they gave her a shot and numbed her breast, and they were going to just cut the edge of the breast, because the lump was up close to the skin.

I was wandering around the Emergency Room crying. I was beside myself. Surely this couldn't happen to me. God wouldn't let this happen to me, but it was happening to me. Mary was my wife, those were my breasts. Yeah, they were on Mary, but they were mine. I just could not understand what was happening, why it was happening. This did not happen to us. We had a good life. I mean we didn't want a lot. We didn't expect a lot. Pay our bills, putz around a little bit, enjoy life, that's really all we wanted, a healthy child, health ourselves. But, no, this wasn't it.

So I wandered around the Emergency Room crying, really devastated, feeling like life had punched me, punched me not only in the gut but in the head, and I didn't know what to expect.

Mary at our Wedding in 1985.

CHAPTER TWO

It's Cancer!

As I was walking around the Emergency Room, I noticed that it was an old one. It was an old hospital built in 1904. They had done some remodeling, but the basic structure was old. I just wandered around the ER, it was not like a modern one, it was an old one that I could walk where ever I wanted to, and I was crying and tears were rolling down my face, and part of me thought I must look like a really big fool. Six feet four inches tall, and probably at the time 260 pounds, and I'm bawling like a two-year-old who lost his balloon.

And through my grief, I seemed to only be able to focus on how old everything around me was. The light fixtures were old, the light switches were old, and the counters were old. This old hospital was consumed in a weird pink and lime-ish green paint scheme in the ER. It still sticks with me. I was just so lost and I was weak, and I just kept wandering, and I felt so hopeless. And then all of a sudden, Dr. Hough opened the door where Mary had been and still was, and he motioned for me to come in, saying that he would be back in a minute.

So I sat down with Mary who had her bra back on and had a bandage over the incision. She looked remarkably resilient and strong and resolved. She still had sort of a deer-in-the-headlight look like she was surprised, but she wasn't like me. She wasn't a basket-case.

Fairly quickly, Dr. Hough came back in, and he said, "Well, we're 95% sure it's cancer. We have to send it off to be analyzed."

But he described it and moved his fingers like he had a little bit of grit in them. And he said when they cut into it; it was gritty, like sand. It was like he still had some of the cancer between his finger and his thumb and he was rolling it around. And we knew he still felt it in his mind like he still had a piece of it. It was just so disturbing, the way he looked.

He felt sincerely bad for us, and I blurted out, "What does that mean? We were going to have more kids. We were just talking about having kids. I mean, Tom's 18 months old. We were going to maybe start trying in a few months."

And Dr. Hough said, "Well, you know, you never say never, but, you know, be happy you've got one."

And I was, however, also devastated. It was another punch. It was another punch from life that knocked me on my ass. I wanted more kids. I was an only child. There was no way on this planet, if I had anything to do with it, that I was going to allow my son to be an only child. It sucks and I just couldn't believe it!

So Mary started asking the doctor, "Well, what does this mean? What happens if it's the worst?"

And she just kept going down that scenario.

"Well, what if this? What if that?"

And when he'd respond to her questions, she'd always take the more negative path. That was Mary. She always, in some ways, looked at the glass as being half empty.

I was the optimist. If the glass was a quarter full. It was a quarter full, it wasn't three-quarters empty to me. So she wanted to know what the odds were, and Dr. Hough was very honest. He told her that the odds weren't good that young. The younger a person was when the cancer started typically meant it was harder to get rid of and it grew faster. She had just turned 26, and it'd been growing since she was 25. It was devastating.

He told us that we were going to be getting appointments probably that coming Tuesday with the surgeons and with the oncologists, and I said, "But you haven't analyzed it yet."

The doctor responded, "No, but we're 95% sure it's cancer. We're rushing it off. We should get it back by Tuesday morning before we do any surgery."

I was stunned. I was totally stunned absolutely stunned into a dream-like state that was becoming a nightmare. That was a Friday afternoon. We should have been looking forward to having fun on the weekend, not dreading this maybe being our last weekend.

That kept going through my mind, "She's going to die. She's got cancer. She's going to die. She's got cancer."

I mean everybody with cancer dies. This could be our last weekend together. What the fuck? I mean I just couldn't believe it. I was just so lost, so hurt, so knocked off my balance that I couldn't believe it. A part of me wanted to fight back, to fight something but there was nothing to fight.

We came home. We had to tell our parents. Mary had to tell hers. I had to tell my mom and dad. My mom and dad knew that we were in the hospital, because they had Tom with them while Dr. Hough wanted us to come up to the hospital and check the lump. So we had them come over.

Mary called her parents and said, "Can you come down here to our house? I have to tell you something." They lived about 20 miles north on their family farm.

I still remember my mom and mother-in-law talking about some of the crazy cures that people would do that my mom read in the those magazines at the front of the checkout counter in the grocery stores, and my mother-in-law read in some health magazine.

So I was very frustrated then. I mean if we were going to beat it, we were going to beat it with science. We were going to beat it with facts. I had gone to college, and I felt like I was fairly smart. Mary was smart. She went to college. You know, we didn't really believe in superstitions. We were religious. We thought surely maybe God can heal us, but we didn't really believe that green tea and broccoli was going to cure her.

When they left, and Mary and I were alone with Tom, we just looked at each other in shock. It was a long weekend. We talked a lot. I talked about how we were going to beat it. She was going to be fine. I was going to keep Mary around and have a 60th wedding anniversary like my Grandpa and Grandma Stalter did. But it wasn't to be.

It was a long weekend. We didn't sleep and snuggled a lot. Didn't have any sex, because let me tell ya, Junior wasn't working on me. Even if Mary'd been in the mood, I couldn't have done it. I was that upset and as a 30-year-old guy who's in pretty good shape from working out, that says a lot about how stress affects "a guy's sex drive."

But all weekend long, Mary kept telling me what to do when she was gone. How to raise Tom, what to do in this scenario, what to do in that scenario, how to clean the house, how to do different things, you know. What to look for in another woman, because I needed somebody, she said. That would be a theme that would get me in a situation that I didn't want to be in down the road.

I finally snapped, I still remember. I was standing in the dining room looking through the two doors in the small hallway straight into the bathroom where Mary was standing in front of the mirror. We were going to go somewhere with Tom. I think it was a Saturday afternoon and she was putting her makeup on, combing her hair, and I finally snapped. I just snapped. I started yelling and screaming and stomping, and I told her to stop talking about her dying, that she wasn't "going to fucking die", that I couldn't deal with it. There was no point in her dying, because I couldn't go on.

27

I just bawled, and I said, "You have to stop it."

She looked at me very calmly. She had a lot of willpower at that time, a lot of strength.

She said, "You need to face the facts. I'm young, this happened, it's not good, and you need to know what to do." And I just sat down and bawled. I cried as hard as I ever did in my life up to that point. I couldn't believe it. I could not believe it.

It was weird - that first weekend that we knew she had cancer, because Mary was strong and I was the weak one. We just were in such shock that this was happening.

On Tuesday, we had the appointment with the surgeons first. They explained what the surgery would be like, and then we went to the oncologists and they explained what the chemo would be like. It was very strange. We felt like we were living in a nightmare.

It wasn't happening, but yet it was and so we got things ready for Wednesday's surgery. The doctors told us on Tuesday afternoon that Mary couldn't eat after a certain time and what to expect and when to be at the hospital in the morning. They were going to operate the first thing. They were in a rush. I noticed that. I felt really strange.

Everybody was in a rush to get Mary into surgery, and I thought, "This isn't good."

I mean, they're not telling us a lot of things, but from working at a maximum security prison and being observant, I knew when things were odd. Even though I felt like I'd had my bell rung with some gorilla wearing brass knuckles. I kept thinking, "Why are they rushing so fast? Why can't we wait a week or two?"

We had it lined up that my Grandpa and Grandma Stalter would come over and watch Tom, because all of the family was going to be up in the waiting room while Mary had surgery. My mom and dad, and some of Mary's family, and we were going to wait there while Mary had surgery.

So with everything arranged, we had that last night at home, Mary was sitting on the loveseat and I was sort of on the floor in front of her, sort of snuggling as much as you can with one person on a loveseat and the other on the floor. I don't even remember what we were watching on TV, then we turned the TV off and talked. Mary started to feel sad, I think for the first time and she said to me as she held her left breast, with her left hand, she said, "This is the last night I'll have this."

29

And then it started to soak in on her that she was afraid I wouldn't love her or I wouldn't want to be with her, that I wouldn't think she was still pretty. It started bothering her and we talked about that.

I still remember looking at her, and she looked back at me, her eyes were welling up with tears, and I said, "You know, it's a boob. Granted, I love it and I like to stick my face between both of them and go, 'Bwoowoowoo,' and, you know, I'd rather have you whole and healthy. But if I can't, I'd still rather have you with one breast gone."

She didn't really believe me, and so I said, "Would you love me any less if I lost my arm or my leg?"

Think about it. We work in a maximum security prison. Shit can happen. We can walk in there one day whole and come out not, you know? The prison had a riot a few years before we started working there, and they tried to cut off some guard's arms and legs with shovels. It was a violent place, and I told her, I said, "You know, seriously, would you love me any less if I lost my arm?"

She said, "No." I said, "Would you love me any less if I lost my leg?" And she said, "No," but she said, "That's different." She said, "My boob is part of me, it's what makes me sexy, what makes you want me."

I said, "You know, I want you because you're you. I want you because of what's inside of you, you know?" I said, "Yeah, losing a boob is traumatic in some ways, but I'm probably still going to be horny for you."

And I said that we would be fine, that we would make it.

So we did. We made it through the night and went to the hospital the next morning.

Tom's 2nd birthday, Mary was undergoing her 1st round of Chemo.

CHAPTER THREE

The Surgery and Effects.

We had the surgery on Wednesday, October 10, 1990, Grandma Stalter's 85th birthday. Mary and I got up early and took Tom over to my parents. They were going to watch Tom for a couple of hours, then bring him back to our house and let my Grandpa and Grandma Stalter and Great Uncle Walter and Great Aunt Ruth watch Tom while Mary had surgery. Uncle Walter was my grandma's brother.

I got prepared to leave. I put the dogs, Isis and Asta, in their crates in the basement, and I didn't want an accident to mess anything up. We went to the hospital for the surgery, started waiting, did the prep, said our good lucks, and reassurances. My mom and dad came up a little later after they had taken Tom back to my house. We were understandably very nervous and had jittery conversations centering around our collective wish that all would go well.

Then the anesthesiologist came to the waiting room and let me know I could go sit with Mary until surgery, so I did. Mary and I just talked about nothing much. She seemed to be a little nervous, and I was still sort of a blubbering idiot! It was sort of funny, because fairly soon our roles would switch. I would become the strong one and

Mary would become the emotional one, which just wasn't like her. Mary was always very guarded with her emotions, feelings, and thoughts. When dating her I couldn't tell if she was having a good time or not, she was as they say a hard read. Even after we got married I couldn't always tell what type of mood she was in. Mary was the type of person who didn't show her emotions and I was very shocked to see her become emotional as time went on.

When Mary was taken away for surgery, I went back to the waiting room and was just very antsy. I couldn't sit still, and I ended up leaving the hospital. I just couldn't stay there. I wasn't a doctor; there was nothing I could do, so I just decided that I had to move around. The walls were closing in on me. My stomach was churning. It felt like knots at the same time that I was being punched in the stomach, and I was nauseous. I wanted to go check on Tom and my grandpa and grandma and see how the dogs were doing.

I had left the hospital before when Mary was in there, and it was when we were having Tom. I guess hospitals bother me. I just can't sit still in them. I can go visit for a little bit, wander around, come back and visit, and wander around. I just can't sit there in the room. I had left for about four hours when Mary was in labor with Tom. I think subconsciously I hoped that she would have Tom while I was gone, and I had used the excuse I had to get some dog food. I was in pretty big trouble when I got back. I wasn't allowed to leave the room until Tom was born, which in itself was quite a story. I guess I just can't handle hospitals.

The idea of being in a hospital means a person is sick and being sick is being weak in my mind. From the time I was able to remember my dad, he was always so very strong and tough. I never felt that I measured up to him or his standards, not that he did anything to make me feel that way. He was a great father and it was my own perception, which I'm not sure how I got.

When Tom was born, I was standing there, in the delivery room and the doctor's getting ready. I remember thinking, "Okay, the doctor's not standing here to catch the kid."

As my son began to emerge from the birth canal, I was getting nervous, and I said something to the doctor and the nurse.

"Oh, it's fine, it's fine."

And it was.

When the obstetrician got there to actually deliver Tom, things were fine. She pulled Tom out and I thought, "Oh, Shit! He's messed up! He's sort of purple and a chalky white."

Then the doctor, because Tom came out face down, couldn't really tell what gender he was. So she spun him around like a baton to get him up in the air to see if he was a little boy or girl. He was a little boy, or at least I thought he was. But he was deformed, I thought. His testicles were flat, he just had a penis.

I thought, "Oh, my God, he's deformed! He's got a cone head, he's purple and white."

I started to pass out. I remember the doctor saying to one of the nurses, "Sit him down," and they shoved me in a chair that was against the wall. The last thing I remember was an oxygen mask about a foot in front of my face, and then I just blacked out. So hospitals don't have terribly positive memories for me, so I left. While Mary's having surgery I wanted to get out of the hospital.

I think that being an only child I feared the day that my parents and grandparents would die. I feared being alone and if I stay out of the hospital I won't be alone. Being an only child is in my opinion a horrible way to grow up. I felt a tremendous amount of pressure to be a little grown up and to act responsibly. To be strong!

When I got back to the hospital, Mary was still in surgery. It seemed like forever, but it probably wasn't much more than about an hour when the doctor came and said she was fine. She was in recovery, and we could go see her in a little bit.

From there on out, things went fairly normally and smoothly for a surgery. She recovered. She was in the hospital a couple of days. They put some drainage tubes in. She seemed to be physically fine.

However, what was surprising to me and actually stunned me looking back on it was that, already, our roles had reversed. Mary was now more in shock. She was weak physically. I think the drainage tubes bothered her. She looked sort of like a Borg from *Star Trek*, and her mental state was different. She was weak, not strong like she had been before the surgery. It was a realization, a bucket of cold water getting thrown on me that it was time for me to suck it up and become the strong one. I needed to carry the burden, and I carried that burden until my dad would die 17 years later. It was a burden that affected me in more ways than I can probably know or explain or describe. But I became the strong one for a long, long time. And it had its effects on me.

Mary seemed to be doing okay, and about a week after surgery, we went to the surgeon's office to pull out the tubes and check her incisions and check her blood pressure, her temperature, listen to her heart and lungs, poke her stomach and look in her mouth, nose and ears. And she was doing fine. She was a little bashful about me seeing the surgical site at first, but it happened. I saw it, and it was quite a surprise in a lot of ways. There was just flat skin. It looked like a belly with a scar. There was no breast, there was no more nipple it was just flat with a scar across it. But as the doctor was pulling out the tubes, it seemed to affect Mary. It didn't really hurt. She didn't complain, but I think she was stunned at how long the tubes were that were in her. It seemed that one tube was probably about eight feet, because they just kept pulling and pulling and pulling, and the more they pulled, the bigger Mary's eyes got and the whiter her face got. So she almost passed out. I was holding her and patting her and telling her it was fine, and she seemed to be okay when he got the tubes out. I think she was a little shocked, though, when he looked at her incision and felt it. It was almost like the realization hit her then that her breast was gone forever.

It was sort of strange though, as time went on, because Mary became different. She was very shy about talking to people at work of her cancer and the surgery and the treatment. Before, she had not been shy. She was always very talkative, very friendly, but she became a little bit withdrawn, and I'm not really sure why, but she did.

Me, on the other hand, I had to talk about it. I had to get it out. It was like a beast. It was like an explosion. It was like diarrhea of the mouth. I had to get it out of me. I could not hold it in. So people would ask, I'd tell them. Sometimes I'd probably volunteer when they didn't really want to ask. But that's just me, and that's why I'm writing this book, so I can let people know now how different people react and how I reacted. I must admit it is hard to admit I was wrong so many times, I did the wrong thing so many times, but I want others to learn from my mistakes, so they won't suffer or have regrets like I do.

I had a couple of bosses at work. One boss was very good. He was retiring and they had made a new position, sort of his assistant, for the guy that was going to take over for him. My old boss, Paul, was very good to me. He said he knew I was worried about being alone, and that I had to do what I had to do, and if it just got to be too much pressure to let him know. He'd have me go get supplies, even supplies in another town 30 miles away, if I just needed a drive.

He said, "If you need to just take a walk around the prison, go out. Do whatever you need to do. I know it's hard."

He once told me that he knew from experience that a lot of people worried greatly over the death or serious illness with a spouse, and he was great.

His replacement, however, was not nearly as good. He called me into his office later that same day or the next day and told me that my work can't slack. He didn't want any excuses, and he had no sympathy. He was heartless towards me at this time in my life. He just told me that he expected me to have the same output at work, the same professionalism, and there were no excuses. What was peculiar was that he seemed to feel no empathy or compassion.

I would have thoughts of being a Rottweiler and biting my replacement boss's neck and ripping it out.

Later in my Corrections career when I would become the Chief Fiscal Officer, I would think of what this guy would do when dealing with subordinates and I would always try to do the opposite of what he would do. Looking back, this was a good learning lesson on why we should have empathy for others, because when someone doesn't show us kindness or have empathy for us, I know how it feels.

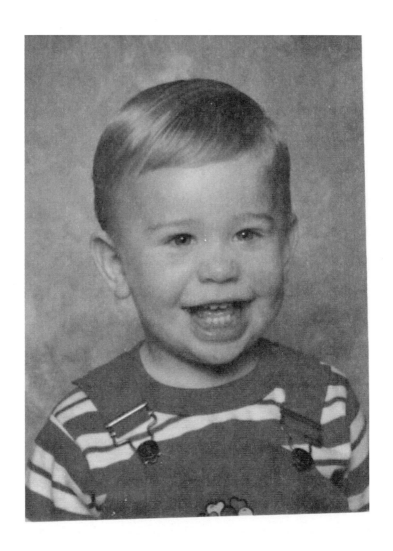

Tom at 18 months.

CHAPTER FOUR

Chemo.

About six weeks after surgery, Mary was back to work. She was feeling pretty good, but the chemo was going to start. It was going to be every three weeks for nine treatments. I remember she was going to get adriamycin, which was a really strong chemo drug, but it was also a very pretty red, the color that you would want a sporty car to be. I was in la-la land at this point. I remember thinking that she came through the surgery. They said they couldn't find any more cancer in her, but they were going to do chemo as a precaution, so I was somewhat guardedly optimistic.

I thought, "Well, maybe she might be all right," and, you know, our life was starting to get maybe a little bit more back to normal, a little bit more relaxed. But the chemo would change that.

Mary and I had started having sex again. She would always wear a tee shirt. She was very shy and embarrassed about me seeing her, and she would not have an orgasm. She just couldn't relax. But I know from talking to Mary, she sort of felt like it was her wifely duty, and she wanted to make me happy and so I thought, "Well, maybe she'll get into it." But it would take her almost a year before she would have an orgasm again.

41

As chemo started in November, we went through the holidays in a strange mindset this time, because Mary had had the cancer. Life seemed much more precarious than it had before. Little did I know that this would be my last good Christmas that I would have for the rest of my life, because in February my Grandpa Stalter got sick. He started feeling a little dizzy one day. He thought he had a touch of the flu. It was a Tuesday. He had been to a Senior Citizens activity the day before, and played cards and had lunch with my grandma. They had enjoyed themselves, and he thought that maybe he ate something that just wasn't quite right.

I ended up talking to him that Tuesday night, and he said he felt like he had a little bit of the flu. It was all right when he laid down, but when he was up, he wasn't doing the best, just felt a little lightheaded. So after I talked to my grandpa and grandma on the phone, I called my dad and told him. The next morning he called and told them that they should take grandpa to the doctor, predicting that it might be his blood sugar's off a little bit. Well, it was his heart.

He was put into Intensive Care on Wednesday afternoon. The electrical impulses in his heart weren't quite right. The heartbeat was off, and I still remember rushing out of work and going to see Grandpa in the hospital. He was just getting in the hospital bed,

42

starting to take his shirt off, and he was scared and that scared me, because my grandpa usually wasn't scared. He was pretty calm, relaxed, knew what was going on, had been through a lot. But I could tell he was really afraid, and he says, "I'm just doing what they're telling me to, Honey." He then reached out and took a hold of my hand and squeezed. I could feel the fear in his grip. Grandpa had always had a vise-like grip, and even on his death bed he still did. I thought this old man is one tough son of a gun.

My grandpa was the type of guy that called everybody he loved "Honey." Men, women, it didn't matter. I guess it's a trait that my dad picked up, and I ended up picking it up, too, because I call my son and the people I care about "Honey" a lot.

Grandpa was in the hospital for a couple days. They were doing tests; trying to figure out what they could do, maybe put a pacemaker in, and then he died in his bed.

Luckily, he was in Intensive Care. They were able to bring him back, but he was never himself again. He would mumble a little bit, but he just wasn't awake or mentally sharp. They took him to a hospital in Springfield, Illinois, that specialized in heart treatments and putting in pacemakers. He was there for about two and a half weeks and, still he died. My grandma stayed with him. I went to my grandpa and grandma's house just about every day and watered Grandma's plants and took care of the mail and made sure the house was ok.

Since Tom was 2 years old by that time and Mary was doing the chemo, I didn't go to and see Grandpa in the Springfield hospital. I always regret that I didn't, but I didn't expect him to die.

Mary had a treatment the day after Grandpa died. She was going to skip it, but both my dad and my Grandma Stalter told Mary, "No, go ahead and get your treatment. Keep on schedule."

They didn't want anything messing it up.

"Life was for the living," they said, and that she needed to live, and that's what Grandpa would've wanted. So Mary missed my grandfather's wake, but she made it to the funeral on that Thursday. We ended up burying Grandpa in the family plot. I was a pallbearer with my other male cousins.

About two weeks later, Grandma wanted to drive again. She had kept her license up, but she really hadn't driven in about a year and a half, since Grandpa had driven all the time. So I went over to see how she was getting along and to help her reacquaint herself with driving. She was 85, almost 86. She took off like she always did and drove around a few blocks in her small little town of Flannigan, and then she said, "Let's go see, Poppy."

44

Poppy was what my Grandma, Dad and Uncle Cal called Grandpa. So out to the cemetery we went. Grandma drove like an old pro.

Mary's schedule was essentially that she went to work, 8-4 Monday through Friday, and on every third Monday she had her chemo treatment. She would stay home the following Tuesday and Wednesday, mostly throwing up, and usually go back to work on Thursday. As time went on, she gradually became more and more tired, and she would go to bed earlier and earlier. It wasn't long before we would get home between 4:30 P.M. and 5:00 P.M. from work, and Mary would eat supper and then be in bed.

I took care of Tom this whole time. I would feed him and bathe him and play with him and do his regular routine. I did his laundry and mine. Mary still didn't trust me doing her laundry. Somehow I had a knack for taking her whites and making them pinks and blues. I also had a knack for making her pinks and blues gray. She would always get mad no matter how pretty of a color I had turned her clothes. Somehow I just couldn't figure out how to do her laundry, but I could do Tom's and mine. Tom, thank God, was a good kid, wasn't fussy, usually in bed sound asleep by about 7:30, which gave me time to train the Rottweilers.

I'd added another dog. I had a male. So I had two female Rottweilers and a male, and I thought, "Well, I could make a little extra money by having puppies, and I certainly enjoy playing with the dogs and training them and taking them to shows."

I had purchased Soko von der Mauth, Schutzhund 3, ZTP, OFA good. He was a show dog, but originally, he'd been a police dog in Germany. Schutzhund is a protection sport, a police dog sport, and Soko had earned titles at the highest level. In fact, his littermate brother was on the German team that won the World Championships in 1990 and placed for several years in a row in Europe in the top three of the World Schutzhund Championships.

Soko didn't really like a lot of people. He was a one-person dog. But he seemed to like me. We got along well. I brought him home to two female dogs that were in heat, and so he was pretty happy with me when he first came to live with us, and so I guess he took to me.

I walked him every night, and he was my buddy. Normally, I wouldn't have been able to get a dog like this, but when Mary was first diagnosed and first starting the treatments, I would walk one of the two female dogs around in the evening. I'd usually end up over at my mom and dad's, who lived about four blocks away. I would sit on their chair or on their couch or sometimes just on the floor and I would cry. I would tell them I was scared that Mary was going to die, that I'd be alone, and I didn't know how to raise Tom. I couldn't manage a household. I knew what I could do, and I knew what I couldn't do, and I couldn't raise a family by myself. My parents were heartbroken. They hated seeing me upset, but I couldn't cry at home.

About two weeks after Mary's surgery, she caught me one day being sort of down, and she said, "What's the matter?"

I responded, "Oh, just everything. I'm worried about you and thinking about having to raise Tom by myself, and it just sort of, ugh, gets to me."

Well, I shouldn't have done that, because Mary ended up crying for about the next five hours. She felt badly that she was doing all this to me.

So I learned I couldn't show negative or sad emotions in front of Mary. I had to shut myself off. I couldn't cry. I couldn't feel bad. I could cry and feel bad but I couldn't cry or feel bad in front of Mary, so I had to do it somewhere safe. The safest place I knew was back at the house I grew up in. The house I'd lived in since I was four with my mom and dad.

One night as I was sitting at my parent's house wiping the tears off my face and blowing the snot out of my nose after a good cry. My mom said, "I wish there was something I could do for you."

And me, being a typical 30-year-old smartass, replied, "Well, there's this dog that's for sale that I'd really like to get. I could breed him with Isis and Asta. Plus I could show him and have fun, and I could stud him out to other females and probably make some money."

My mom and dad both questioned, "How much is he?"

"He's priced at $5,000."

My dad was rolling his eyes and saying, "There's no way," and my mom said, "That's a lot of money."

The next day my mom called me up at work. "Well, if you can get the guy to go to $4,500, I'll give you the money, we can split the stud fees that you get off of him, and that way you can pay me back."

So my mom bought me a toy, a $4,500 toy that I think, in some ways, kept me sane through those days, because Soko was such a cocky, upbeat, positive-type of dog that he helped me make it through a lot of shit and hard times.

He wasn't scared of anything. Somehow his courage and his confidence radiated into me, and those qualities still do today, even as I write this book. When I get down or frustrated or depressed, I think

48

of Soko and how he used to walk in a beautiful bouncing prance up on his toes. He wasn't scared of anything. He would've taken on the world. In fact, I used to joke that Soko would take on an Army tank, even if knew he was going to lose.

I worked him in the sport of Schutzhund, and he seemed to astound everybody with how smart he was. In fact, we went high in trial for Protection in the one trial I showed him at. We ended flunking Obedience, because he wanted to do what he wanted to do, and I wasn't a good enough dog trainer. But he just did really well in Protection and tracking work.

That first summer that I had Soko after Mary had finished her chemo, I remember walking him one night. I was still worried about Mary and couldn't sleep. It was probably 1:30 or 2:00 in the morning. So I took Soko for a walk on one of those really hot nights in June where it's humid and voices can be heard for blocks.

As I walked down the street, on the sidewalk, there were three 20-somethings a couple blocks away when I saw them. They were smoking cigarettes, talking fairly loud, and every other word was a cuss word. By the time they noticed me about a block away I could hear everything they were saying. They didn't see Soko. It's sort of hard to see a black dog at night, especially when they're about knee

49

high or so. I heard these guys say, "Well, there's somebody walking. We're going to make the fucker move off the sidewalk."

They talked and they joked and they were going to say this and that and they were pretty cocky and thought they were going to intimidate me. Not that they would have, even without Soko, but with Soko, I couldn't help but smile.

I gave Soko the command to pay attention, "Pass auf!" Not quite "piss off," but it sounds like "piss off." "Pass auf!"

As they got closer and closer, I think they realized that I had a dog, because they started walking a little slower, and then pretty soon I heard them say, "He's got a dog."

By the time they got about 10 feet in front of me, they said, "Sir, does your dog bite?"

I responded, "Well, he's a trained police dog. He only bites if I tell him to."

It was sort of funny, because, as a group they parted and let me keep walking right down the sidewalk. I couldn't help but smile, even to this day, thinking, "Yep, they were going to make me get off the sidewalk, but yet they got off the sidewalk."

One of my favorite stories of this time period involves a couple of friends who came over to play cards with Mary and me. Kendy, who has been a very dear friend, that I love like a sister for 20 plus years, and her boyfriend at the time dropped by. Kendy and Mary were partners and Kendy's boyfriend and I were partners. Tom was asleep and Kendy wanted me to bring one of the Rottweilers into the room where we were playing cards so she could see one.

I brought Soko in, gave him a rawhide chew and told him to lie down next to me. He was between Kendy and me.

She wanted to be his friend and was talking to him. However, Soko didn't want to be talked to. He just wanted to eat his rawhide chew and relax. He growled a couple of times and Kendy laughed a little, thinking it was cute. I told her to stop because he just wanted to chill, but she kept talking to him.

Finally he stopped chewing his rawhide and stood up, took a step or two towards Kendy and showed his teeth and growled very firm and loud. Then he turned away picked up his rawhide chew and laid back down. Only now he was facing away from Kendy. He was a smart dog.

So my mom and Soko helped me out and kept me sane.

One more life preserver in this sea of despair. One more clip of bullets in this war against cancer. Soko was a great dog. About a year after that, he got prostate cancer, and we had to put him to sleep.

He died in my arms, and I thought that I would be strong; after all, he was only a dog. I'd been through everything with Mary. She was getting healthy. We were hopeful that she would be cured, but as I held Soko and felt him go limp in my arms, I didn't cry in the Vet's office. I had learned to shut my tears off on command, but I couldn't talk. I carried Soko out to the car and then that night my dad and I took him out to the family farm, and we buried him in the pet cemetery that my great-grandfather had started for the family pets. I had lost my buddy and a companion, my wingman. Soko was more than a dog.

My grandparents, Lester & Cleo Stalter.

CHAPTER FIVE

Sarah, My Little FU to Cancer.

Mary was done with chemo in May of 1991, and I was joking with her that she wouldn't have any more of that punk hairstyle. I told her I didn't know if I could get excited and make love to her if she didn't have punk hair. She laughed. But I could tell she realized that we both wanted her hair to grow back and be normal. But, you know, sometimes we just had to joke about those things or we'd cry. We did a lot of that, or at least I did a lot of crying. Mary almost didn't get her last two rounds of chemo; it was hitting her so hard. She had gotten in the habit of getting her chemo on Monday night after work, taking Tuesday and Wednesday off, but it was getting to the point the last few chemo treatments were causing her to feel terrible on Thursday and Friday.

But she did it. She toughed it out and she got the last two chemo treatments for the whole series, and then the oncology team did some scans and some blood work. She didn't seem to have any trace of cancer, so we thought maybe we were out of the woods. Hopefully, life would be good. We'd lost my grandpa in March, and my Grandma Stalter would stay with my mom and dad three or four nights a week, and then she'd stay at her house two or three days out of the week. Once in a while she would stay at our house with Mary, Tom and me. She kept telling us that she was going to move to Pontiac and live next door to my mom and dad before winter came. But that wasn't going to happen.

My grandma had taken a trip to see my uncle and aunt in Texas and all my cousins around the middle of June. She got back towards the end of June and within a few days of getting back, she had a brain aneurism. She was in a coma for about three days and then she passed. She happened to be talking to an old friend, a lifelong friend that she'd known for about 50 years. They were both widows, and my grandma's last few words were to her friend, Ada, was that it's a shame you can't go with your spouse. You know, you're together and then you're not. They had said a few more words and then all of a sudden my grandma's head leaned over on her shoulder and her tongue just stuck out of her mouth, and she had had an aneurism, just that simple, just that quick, just that painless.

She'd always wanted to go that way, just quick and easy, no pain, no knowing about it, just boom, you're gone. I heard stories all of my life that my great-grandma, Grandma Stalter's mom, passed away in her sleep. Quick, easy and painless, everyone's way to die if they could pick. The last few years, Grandma Stalter always said she didn't want to go alone, but she didn't want to die in front of family and scare them. So she had a stroke in front of her friend and scared the shit out of her. Ada ended up running out the front door screaming and hollering. Luckily, there were some construction guys putting a new roof on a house just a couple houses away. They called 911 because Ada wasn't clear-headed enough at the time to call 911. Grandma made it to the hospital, but she never woke up.

One of the hardest things I think my dad ever had to do was to follow the doctor's advice and pull the plug on my grandma. Even though she didn't die when we pulled the plug, it was one of those things where we knew she was going to die, and I'd never seen my dad struggle so much. As my grandma was dying, my father told my grandma to tell Grandpa "Hi".

She had been unresponsive all the way through her stay in the hospital, but she had a few more breaths left in her and a big tear rolled down her cheek before she died when dad said "Tell Poppy hi."

We had the visitation a few days later, July 2, and that was really the last time that my dad and my uncle, my mom, my Aunt Mary, my Mary, me, and all my cousins were together, because a few months after that, my Aunt Mary would also die. Life is sort of funny that way. You just never know when it's going to be over. Forrest

Gump has it right when he said, "Life was like a box of chocolates. You never know what you're gonna get."

Within a few months of my grandma dying we got her house cleaned up and the household items sold off. My dad and my uncle divided the assets between them, split the 40 acres, got a tenant lined up and did all the estate tasks you do to clean up an estate.

Things were pretty much normal for Mary and me for the next four years. She seemed to be in remission, and life was pretty good. We did the regular family activities, but there was always a cloud, always that gnawing, chewing, scratching, tickling fear that the cancer would come back. We knew the statistics, we knew the odds. They appear to be much worse now, but they weren't good back then for reoccurrence of cancer.

My family doctor who I really loved and still do, even though he retired, pissed me off a few times, because when I'd get my yearly physical (I had started getting them every year since Mary got sick), he'd always tell me, "You know, you need to take care of yourself. Mary's cancer is going to come back."

I had gotten into weightlifting. I couldn't jog anymore, because my knees couldn't take the pounding and I was putting on the pounds. He kept getting on me to take the weight off, to do more cardio, and not worry about being strong. However, I'd always felt that for a guy that was 6'4" I wasn't as strong as I should be for my size. But with lifting weights, even though I started looking like a big fatty, I was getting really strong. I was curling weights that I hadn't curled before. I was bench pressing weights I hadn't pressed before. In a lot of ways, I felt really good about myself. I was still doing Tae Kwon Do, still doing some cardio, but I just didn't look like an athlete. I felt like one, didn't look like one, so I didn't care, I felt good.

But a few times, Dr. Hough would tell me, "You need to take care of yourself, because that cancer's going to come back,"

And it did, but it still pissed me off when he would say it. I knew it was true, but yet, I kept thinking, "Don't tell me that shit. I don't want to hear it, you know? I want to stick my head in the sand and believe that the fairytale's going to last forever."

But as time went on, Mary would say things like "It's going to come back, it's going to get me," and it would upset me. We even had a few fights over it.

One night she was watching TV and I came in from doing something. I remember sitting down next to her, snuggling up because I always have been a snuggler, I guess, and I asked her what she was watching. It was some story about a mom or a wife

57

who was dying of cancer. One of those made-for-TV movies, and I just got up and I said, "I'm not watching this. I'm going to go do something else,"

She got mad at me and told me I needed to watch it, because it was going to happen to us.

I responded, "You know, it's not going to happen to us." and we went back and forth like that for a while.

She told me that I needed to face my fears, that it was going to happen, and sooner or later, sometime at one of the doctor's appointments he was going to tell us the cancer was back.

I did my typical things when I was mad and fighting with Mary. I'd stomp around like a two-year old and slam doors. Not that it really did a lot of good, but it sort of made me feel better. It probably looked pretty stupid, too, but that's what I did. I didn't believe in hitting a spouse. I never hit Mary. I think the worse thing I ever did was throw a pillow at her one time. I didn't mean to hit her with it and I'm glad it didn't hurt her. But, no, I think that if you're a big, tough guy and you want to prove how much of a stud you are, you don't hit women, you know? Maybe go down to the biker bar and pick a fight with somebody bigger than you, but you don't hit women. Mary and I had a pretty good fight that night and didn't talk a lot for a couple days, but we got over it.

I didn't really want to watch anything with dying in it. I didn't want to feel worried about the future. I just wanted to have life keep going the way it was. In fact, life got better for a while.

I still remember the night that Mary and I conceived our daughter, Sarah. It was one of those nights that she started behaving amorously.

I'm thinking, "Okay, this is sort of cool."

We had to be careful, because it hadn't been five years since she was done with chemo. We had talked to the doctors about having another child. They said it was possible, but not to even try or think about it until Mary'd been off of chemo and cancer-free for five years. They kept telling us we were young enough not to worry about it, so we didn't worry about it as far as thinking about having a kid went. We simply thought that if we had another child, we had another child. It would be a blessing. If we didn't, we had one child already and we were happy with that and we had each other.

But that night, I wore the protection, because Mary couldn't take birth control pills. The hormones in them could trigger the cancer again according to the doctors. Even though they had given her birth control pills when she was taking the chemo in order to protect her ovaries, they didn't want her taking the birth control pills now.

So I put a "raincoat" on, and I didn't take care of business for Mary. Since she's the one that started it, I told her, "Okay, well, we can wait 15 or 20 minutes and try again."

And as a typical husband will do, and few men will probably admit, I put the raincoat back on 15 or 20 minutes later and struck out again. I didn't take care of business! I felt bad and Mary was a little frustrated.

She said to me, "You know, we're going to do this right before we're done."

So we laid there and cuddled for a while and talked and relaxed, and before long, I was ready to get in the batter's box again. She told me not to worry about a raincoat, because it wasn't that time of the month. We were safe and I could always pull out.

Well, things don't always work as planned, and it seemed like—I guess the best way to put this is, she hit her homerun the same time I hit my homerun, so that's when Sarah was conceived.

That was the only time that we did anything without protection, and it was a blessing. It's a blessing that would save my life later on. Even if it wasn't five years after Mary got done with chemo, it was four and a half years, so we were close to what the doctors wanted.

The strange thing is that night after I fell asleep snuggling with Mary, I dreamed about my Grandma Stalter. I had had a couple dreams about her, real vivid dreams. I was very close to my Grandma Stalter. It was right after she had died. I dreamed that she had come back to tell me goodbye, because I didn't get to tell her goodbye.

My grandpa sort of lingered in the hospital and I was able to tell him goodbye.

However, Grandma was just like a light switch—out. Grandma came back in a dream. It was the most real dream I think I'd had in my life up to then. I didn't understand what it was. But I truly believe it was her spirit coming back to tell me goodbye, and we talked a little bit and hugged. She told me to watch Tom and Mary and my mom and dad the first time she came to me in a dream. The second time I dreamed about my grandma that vividly, I got an ass-chewing.

It was very hard for me to move on from her and grandpa's death. We'd had the house sale for my grandparent's household goods, and I want to say just about every day the grief seemed like it was overwhelming me. The walls were closing in, and my grandpa and grandma were gone. Even though I had Mary and Tom and my parents, my grandpa and grandma had always been a huge part of my life.

I had a weird dream that I wandered through my grandparents' house after the sale. The house was empty and bare. When it was still up for sale, and I'd actually done that a few times, just wandered through the house reminiscing, remembering days gone by, happy times, and fun times.

In my dream, I was walking into my grandpa and grandma's bedroom as my grandma walked out of their bathroom. It was an older-style farmhouse that we could actually run circles around inside the house. One could walk in the front door, turn to the right and go to the living room. Then there was a door going into the kitchen. Then, a door going into the bathroom. Then another door from the bathroom going into their bedroom, and then back to the front hallway.

So, in my dream, as I walked into my grandpa and grandma's bedroom that was bare, completely empty of everything. There was one old sweater of my grandmother's still hanging on the back of the bathroom door. The bathroom door opened and out came my grandma.

I greeted her by saying, "Hi, Grandma. I'm glad to see ya!"

She replied that she was glad to see me and she loved me, but that I needed to get over her and grandpa's death.

I needed to move on, that that was just the way life was. She talked just like she normally did.

"There, there, now, now, here, here."

She wasn't an educated woman, but she was smart. She didn't have the best English, but she communicated well, and she told me, in effect, that this was life. Parents and grandparents are supposed to go before kids and that we all go on. We go on for the next generation.

She told me not to be sad that she and my grandpa weren't there for my birthday, because I had found my present when we were cleaning up the house. My grandparents always bought my presents—well, I think they bought everybody's presents early, usually several months early, and if my grandfather had his way, he usually gave the presents out a month or two before a birthday or Christmas. That was just him and I've sort of inherited that trait. So Grandma told me that I had gotten my present, and I needed to move on.

I never dreamed about her again until that night that Mary and I conceived Sarah. It was very uncanny. I dreamed that my grandma came to me, and I can't even picture the location, but it was Grandma telling me that Mary was going to have a baby and it wasn't going to be a boy.

That's how she talked. Instead of saying it was going to be a girl, she said, "It's not going to be a boy."

When Mary and I had talked about having more children, I always wanted a boy. Girls sort of scared me. I had a boy. I knew how to raise a boy. I was a boy; I knew what to do with boys.

Girls? Shit, what the hell do you do with them? I had enough trouble dating girls, much less raising one. But that was what my grandma said. She said that Mary was going to have a baby and it's not going to be a boy.

The next morning when we woke up, Mary was in the bathroom getting ready for work and I was running around doing something. I said, "Oh, by the way, I had a curious dream last night."

Mary asked, "What was that?"

So I told her, and she started laughing and she replied, "Yeah, right. It's not the right time of the month."

She also reminded me that it was the third time I was up to bat. So we didn't think about it until a little later and Mary missed her period.

Mary ended up being pregnant, and it was a pretty uneventful pregnancy. The thing that I really remember is Mary was just ecstatic. She was really, really happy. It seemed like our life was back on track and, for a little while anyway, the cancer cloud was gone. In some ways it was and in some ways it wasn't. But it wasn't quite as closed in or as dark or as blotting out the sun, maybe, as that cancer cloud had been before.

All through the pregnancy Mary was pretty excited. Things were going well, and as time went on, she was looking more and more forward to having our daughter. We did an ultrasound and the doctors were pretty sure that we were going to have a girl. I remembered thinking, "Oh, my goodness, Grandma was right!"

Mary woke up one morning toward the end of the term and didn't quite feel right. She wasn't sure if she was in labor or not, because Tom had been induced a couple weeks early, but Mary thought she might be in labor. The unexpected and most awesome thing about Mary was she was a little trooper. She said she had to go into work, because there were a couple of memos she had to do.

So Mary went into work, apparently in labor, as it would turn out. A little bit of a funny story to that—a few years later, Mary was up for a promotion. She was being interviewed by a couple of the senior staff members, one who is now the Warden at the prison, and they asked her, "Why should we promote you? What qualities do you have that the other candidates don't have?"

And without missing a beat, Mary said, "I'm the only one that ever came into work to finish a job when I was in labor," and they both laughed, and Mary ended up getting the job.

So, on January 5, 1995, Sarah was born at about 5:35 P.M. I wasn't going to pass out again this time, so I was standing at the edge of the room, sort of peeking around the door. A couple of the nurses were there that had been there with Tom, and they kept looking over at me, "Are you okay? Are you okay?" and I was fine.

Mary wanted to do everything with Sarah since she felt that she'd missed out on about a year and a half with Tom due to her surgery and chemo treatments. The strange thing was that, after Mary was sick, Tom really didn't go to Mary anymore.

I remember one specific time that always pops into my mind. Mary had just finished up with chemo and we were visiting family standing outside. Tom had fallen and scraped his knee, and he was crying. Mary was standing between me and Tom—Tom was probably 20-25 feet away from me, and Mary was right in the middle. As Tom got up I said something to him, and I think Mary said something to him, too, about being okay. Tom stood and his little legs were just a churning. He ran right by Mary and into my arms. Mary didn't say anything but she looked sad, and I could tell it bothered her. A little later that night, she did tell me it bothered her. But I guess that's what happens when you miss out on your child's life when they're between a year and a half and two and a half or three.

Mary wanted to do more with Sarah than she had been able to with Tom. She didn't mind doing the extra stuff that we had split with Tom. She just wanted to catch up on that time. She relished this time much more of holding Sarah in front of the TV or feeding her or just doing every day tasks that she didn't really seem to be able to do with Tom. She had been busier, more worried about cleaning the house or cooking a meal when Tom was a baby. However, with Sarah, Mary just really wanted to hold Sarah. Tom and I could fend for ourselves, and that was fine. It didn't bother me at all.

When Dad retired, Sarah was about a year and a half, a year and three-quarters old. She wasn't quite two yet. Mom had babysat both Tom and Sarah since they were about six weeks old, and when Dad retired, for some reason, he took over dealing with Sarah, and Mom did stuff with Tom. I think part of it was that Mom had started out with Tom, and in some ways, my mom had raised me, so I think she felt a little more comfortable with a boy. Maybe she was just used to Tom. I don't know. But somehow, Sarah seemed to become Dad's and Tom became Mom's. Sarah called Dad Poppa and Dad called Sarah his little "Poppa Monster."

Life was good. We seemed to be going along pretty well. Sarah was two. Mary was down to once a year with the cancer checkup. We'd actually gotten a bigger life insurance policy on Mary, and somehow that made me feel more secure. I always felt that if one had a big insurance policy on somebody, they wouldn't die. I don't know, maybe the old insurance agents in heaven would lobby God to not let the covered person die so their insurance company didn't have to pay out a big settlement. I don't know, but I did feel better.

Things went smoothly for a while, about another year, then Mary went in on March 8, 1999, for her yearly checkup.

I still remember the day clearly. We left work and grabbed a newspaper out of the newspaper stand. Mary wanted something to read while she was waiting to see the doctor. We began talking as we drove a few more blocks, and somehow I drove off with the newspaper when she got out. I was going to run a couple of errands and then pick her up. We weren't worried about anything. I drove half a block before I saw it, thinking, "Oh, crap. Here's the newspaper." So with the one-way streets and the way the town was set up, it took me a couple blocks to get back to the doctor's office, and it was snowing out. I mean there was a good snowstorm. It was almost like a mini-blizzard, and as I walked in I thought, "Man, is it snowing."

After I walked in the doctor's office I looked up and I saw the secretary who was my old principal's wife. In a small town, you seem to know everybody. Then there was a nurse that we had known from the very beginning of Mary's cancer treatment.

They both looked at me very strangely, and I said, "Mary forgot the newspaper. Where's she at?"

"She's already in the examination room."

"Oh, okay. Well, I'll take the paper to her."

"Well, yeah, you need to go in there."

It struck me as out of the ordinary, but I had no fear of anything. I thought things are fine. "Sarah's four now. Mary's been cancer-free for a long time."

As I walked to the exam room, I opened the door and Mary was sitting there in the examination table with this look of stunned disbelief on her face. Our oncologist, Dr. Jeong who is an excellent, excellent oncologist was with her. He looked up at me with a sad face.

I said, "What's wrong?"

He told me that Mary's cancer count was up to 130. A normal cancer count for a person without breast cancer is typically 0-30 when the blood test is run.

So Mary's was really, really high. Apparently Sarah wasn't my little FU to cancer anymore, because the cancer had come back.

Dr. Jeong made some appointments for Mary to get X-rayed. He wanted her checked very soon, and so it seemed like the cancer was back. We hoped it was just a fluke but deep down inside we both knew this was the beginning of the end. When cancer comes back it's usually a death sentence.

Mary's 33rd birthday with Sarah August, 1997.

CHAPTER SIX

Transplant and the Beast.

Mary had to go get some x-rays over the next day or two and what we saw wasn't good. It seemed like her whole lungs were covered in cancer. We weren't really sure what was going on and so Mary had some exploratory surgery. What had happened was the breast cancer had spread to Mary's lungs, and the surgeon described it as if you took a deflated football and dunked it in a bucket of oily slime and pulled it out. There would just be a thin covering of that oily slime on the outside of the football. And that's how Mary's lungs were. There was just a thin covering of cancer over the whole of the lungs. And so we had an appointment to go to the oncologist and see what was going on and see what our options were.

The drive to the appointment was pretty somber at first. Mary had been crying, and like I said before, that wasn't like her. She wasn't a crier and she wasn't an emotional, moody woman. She didn't cry at all during both pregnancies. She seldom cried when we had an argument. I think maybe once or twice in our married lives did she cry when we had an argument. Usually she'd just get mad and grumpy and not talk and sort of shut down and I would do the very mature thing of stomping around, hollering a little bit and slamming a few doors and then going outside. On the drive to the doctor's office, which was about a 40-minute drive, I tried to talk and take Mary's mind off of the upcoming appointment. At first it wasn't working, and then as we got going a little farther, she started talking, and we were doing the what ifs, both the good and the bad, and then we got joking about different things. By the time we were about two-thirds of the way to the doctor's office, Mary was laughing. I think it was one of the hardest things I ever had to do, but somehow I'd cheered her up. She even talked about it. We were saying how it was so strange that we were going to this doctor's appointment about her cancer coming back, knowing the cancer has metastasized, had gone into to her lungs, and yet we were laughing and joking.

And she gave me a good compliment, saying that I was probably one of the only people on the planet that could do that for her.

So we sat down with the doctors, and talked and we were given some options. Mary's oncologist's suggestion was that we do three or four chemo treatments at his office, very strong, knock the cancer down to where we can't see it anymore in the scans, and it's just microscopic, and then we do a bone marrow transplant, which at the time was experimental for breast cancer. The theory was that the patient would be given a massive dose of chemo so strong that it kills the bone marrow, but it also kills all the breast cancer cells. The bone marrow really had nothing to do with the breast cancer. It was such a strong chemo treatment that it would actually kill the bone marrow but before the chemo, the oncology team would have to take out bone marrow from Mary, then give her that massive dose of chemo, a nuclear blast as I called it, and the doctor seemed to agree it was a nuclear blast. Then a few days after the chemo, they would put Mary's bone marrow back into her and, hopefully, it would start growing again.

The bone marrow transplant itself was not so much the worry. The worry was if she had this massive dose of chemo and any if the cancer survived, it would essentially become immune to any other chemo. And with the bone marrow destroyed, Mary was at risk of infection. So this was sort of like going for a homerun or a strikeout.

I did ask for other options, and I was told that the oncologists could give Mary three or four, maybe five, really strong chemo doses, knock the cancer down so it couldn't be seen, and then when it came back in a year or two years, we'd have to repeat the procedure. The theory was that Mary could probably survive 10-15 years doing that, but if she did the bone marrow, she had maybe a 20%-30% chance of an absolute cure. And that's what Mary wanted. I didn't really want that. We would talk about that later, Mary and I, but at that moment, Mary wanted to go for the homerun. The last few days that Mary was alive I told her that I regretted not trying to talk her out of the bone marrow transplant. She was very understanding and told me all it would have done was to make her mad. She would have done it anyway and that I shouldn't beat myself up about it now.

I was worried that it wouldn't work and that she would be dead sooner. If the cancer came back, it would go fairly fast according to the doctor and she might have two to four years. So as I thought about Sarah only being four at the time, if Mary was able to live an additional 10 to 15 years, as compared to two or four, I wanted the sure thing. But Mary wanted to gamble and so gamble's what we did.

We ended up going up to Loyola at Chicago where they had the Bone Marrow Transplant Center. Getting there in itself was an ordeal. The insurance that we had through work somehow didn't want to allow Mary to go to Loyola. The insurance company offered her Sloan-Kettering in New York, Duke in North Carolina, or Anderson in Texas, which didn't make a lot of sense. So we appealed and we fought, and we made a lot of calls. Then finally, based on the contract with the State of Illinois, since we were working at the Pontiac

Correctional Center and the specialist wanted to send Mary to Loyola, the insurance company had to pay for it.

When we got to Loyola, it was a humungous hospital. Coming from a small rural town like Pontiac, Illinois, Loyola in Chicago was just big. In some ways, it was a little intimidating, although I was getting to the point where I was just becoming angry. There was something inside of me that I didn't understand at that time. When I'd get mad I would have thoughts of doing things that were violent and doing things I knew were wrong. It was almost like I thought about being an inmate or doing the things that the inmates did to get in to prison. When someone would make me mad, I'd somehow envision just punching them in the nose or punching them in the stomach. I started having thoughts like this, and I wasn't really sure why I was so frustrated.

I wasn't mad at God. I knew that God was the only hope, and I knew I had to keep my faith in God. I was asking God a lot of whys and I wasn't getting a lot of answers.

Because of this, I was surprised by the size of Loyola and being in the city and it wasn't probably the best neighborhood. As we would find out later, we were told not to go walking out in the parking

76

lot by ourselves at night, but rather to ask for a security guard to escort us to our car.

Upon arriving at Loyola, we were met by a nurse who gave tours to prospective transplant patients. We got the whole tour and it was very impressive. It was almost like something from *Star Trek*, in that the machines and the equipment and the monitoring devices were very elaborate. For a nonmedical person, it was like, "Good, God Gerty, this place is really advanced."

The thing that struck me, though, as we were finishing up our tour, was that the nurse, in probably the most businesslike and impersonal type of tone, said something that was the coldest thing I think I've ever heard in my life, certainly up to that point but possibly even now 12 years later. She looked at Mary and me and said that this is what we would go though, but only if the insurance would cover it or we had $98,500 cash.

I was stunned. I said, "What do you do with people that don't have insurance or the money?"

She replied coldly, "We don't treat them."

I thought right then and there that something was wrong when this country and the people don't care about trying to cure somebody, especially a young mother of two kids.

77

What do you tell those kids? "Gee, mommy didn't have the money so she died," or "Mommy didn't have the money so we didn't fix her."

You know, what do those people do that run the hospitals, that run the insurance companies, that even run the government? Do they go home and tell their kids when they make decisions on life or death. "There was this poor person that didn't have any money so they died," or "We didn't help them."

It was a life-changing event for me right there. My anger boiled up and it seemed like something, a beast, inside of me had broken out. I was angry. I had felt this gnawing anger before, but it was as if something had hatched inside of me, and years later I understood what happened at that time.

To quote the Rocky Balboa movie where he's talking to his brother-in-law about his wife having died of cancer and that there was a "beast inside" of him, I felt at that time, looking back, that there was a beast born within me, not an evil beast, not a beast that wanted to fight against God, but a beast that was angry.

Maybe the best way to describe it was a Christian beast, a beast that was like a knight in the Middle Ages that could be ferocious and vicious and cruel to its enemies, yet merciful and kind to those who didn't pose a threat or who weren't its enemies.

I just remember looking at this nurse thinking, "What in the hell? Do you not have a conscience? You just say that so cold and matter of fact."

It was just a life-changing experience.

But luckily, the insurance was covering us, and we told the nurse that.

Again in a very cold and unfeeling voice, she said, "Well, we need to have the approval letter before we can start the procedure."

We explained to the nurse that we had another chemo treatment or two to do before we would be returning to Loyola, and we left.

About this same time we found a house that was just across the street from the house we lived in at the time. It was a prairie style Frank Lloyd Wright house. An older lady had lived there. She had gone to the nursing home, and the house was for sale. I had fallen in love with the house a few years before when I had helped the lady that lived there do some things. When Mary helped her, she found the house very nice, too. It had wooden built-in bookshelves in the living room with leaded-glass doors. It had two fireplaces. It was

79

about 3,600 square feet, if you counted the basement, probably about 2,400 square feet of living space between the main floor and the upstairs. It had a built-in buffet with leaded glass doors in the dining room. The living room and the dining room had a picture rail. The house was perfect except for the kitchen which would need remodeling. That was the house that Mary and I settled on.

Returning to the timeline, as we were getting ready to go to Loyola for Mary's admission, I was going to drive Mary to her parents, and her parents and her sister were going to drive her to Loyola. Mary had to be there for a couple of days for tests before they actually started removing her bone marrow, and then after an approximate two week stay, the doctors would start doing the chemo.

On that morning, we woke up at 3:30 to take Mary to meet her parents, and she got ready and was putzing around with her baggage. I was doing some things around the house, and I was beside myself. I had a pit in my stomach. Somehow I felt that Mary would never come back from this bone marrow transplant, that she was going to die up there. I felt like throwing up, my stomach was in knots, my head was buzzing, and my arms were tingly. I felt that I had just had the shit beat out of me, and then Mary stunned me.

She came out of the bathroom without any clothes on, grabbed me and pulled me to the couch and started getting fresh. And I'm like, "Whoa, what are you doing?"

She said, "I'm not going to be here for a long time. We need to do this."

I questioned, "What?"

She answered, "Yeah, we need to do it. I won't be here for three or four months and we can't do anything for even a while when I get back. So this is it, I'm trying to take care of you."

The hardest thing I ever did was to make love to Mary that morning. I seem to always have been unable to perform when I was nervous or scared. When I had lost my virginity to Mary, it took a couple weeks before things worked right. We tried three or four times a week for a couple weeks, and I was just scared, which is sort of silly. Here I am 6'4", wrestled in high school and college, boxed a little bit in college, worked at a maximum security prison, and I couldn't perform because Mary was going to Loyola. It was just hard. I think it was the hardest thing I did in my life up to that point. But somehow in my mind I knew that Mary wanted this and if I didn't make love to her, if I couldn't perform she would feel badly. I think in retrospect it was probably the least satisfying sexual experience I ever had in my life.

We made love on the couch and then we got ready to take Mary to meet her parents so that they could drive on up to Loyola. I would see Mary in a few more days, and after I dropped her off, I was going to go to work that day and stay with the kids.

A few days after Mary's admission, I drove there to see her and to find out how she was doing. I hung out with her and her family and talked to the doctors a little bit. It was very surreal. It was as if this wasn't happening to me, and I look back and I think it wasn't happening to me, it was happening to Mary. But in reality, it was happening to me, and at the time, I felt guilty about thinking that. We were married, we were a couple, so what happened to one happened to the other.

Maybe I wasn't the one having the needles stuck in me and pulling out bone marrow and sticking medicine in me, but it was happening to me, and I was angry. That beast inside of me was getting madder and madder and madder, and it was puzzling. I just felt so discouraged and angry. But, as I mentioned before, I wasn't angry at God. I thought, "Well, hopefully, if I keep my faith in God and I keep praying and I keep reading the Bible, somehow maybe He'll change His mind. Maybe He won't take Mary from me."

And on the weekend before Mary had her actual high dose of chemo, the hospital said it would be okay if she went to the zoo. So we took Tom and Sarah to Brookfield Zoo, and that was the last time in almost three and a half months that they would see their mom. They would talk to Mary on the phone just about every night, but it wasn't the same. I sincerely thought she was going to die there at Loyola. I went up there three and four times a week, usually two or three times during the week and then on either Saturday or Sunday, or if I only went twice in a week, I'd go both Saturday and Sunday.

At this time I had a different boss. Being the head of the business office, the Chief Fiscal Officer, was stressful. Bosses lasted two or three years and they moved on. The stress was quite a bit as I would find out later when I took over the job. But the boss I had when Mary was getting her bone marrow transplant told me that I needed to take a leave of absence, because he couldn't plan work around the fact that I was gone two or three days a week. It didn't really matter to him that I had literally 150 sick days on the books. It was inconvenient for him because I was the Assistant Chief Fiscal Officer, I was the Business Manager. It was amazing to me that, at that time, people would say some of the strangest things. Some comments were unbelievably kind and heartfelt and they touched me, and others were the most insensitive, hurtful things that one can imagine. It was at this time that I became angry. My anger was just really busting out.

I also did something else stupid at that time. In the course of lifting weights, being about 280-290 pounds and bench pressing 340 pounds, I started to take some supplements. These supplements became famous when some professional baseball players used them. I didn't know if it would help me hit homeruns, but it certainly seemed to help me lift weights better and get to that 340 that was my max. I started taking Androstene, and I noticed that even though I was only sleeping two to three, maybe if I was lucky, four hours a night, I could still have enough energy to go on. The Androstene seemed to give me energy, but it also made me, in some ways, a raging beast, a raging explosive ready to explode, or as somebody once put it, "a loose cannon that was going to shoot off."

I was angry and the anger was building up, and the longer I was alone at the house without Mary, the angrier I got. It was also at this time another voice started popping up in my head which, for lack of a better phrase, I would call a serene voice, a serene Christian voice that would say to that beast voice, "You know, you really shouldn't be angry. You really shouldn't do this. You really shouldn't drive aggressively. You shouldn't have the road rage," or whatever I was going through.

Many times when I drove up to see Mary, I would think, "I'm just going to tailgate this guy" or "I'm going to cut in front of him."

It's not something I look on and am proud of. It's just that it happened, and the stress and the pressure of work, of thinking that my wife's going to die, of raising and dealing with two small kids by myself, was overwhelming. I really couldn't handle it. The truth of the matter is men are the weaker sex. Some men are or perhaps more capable than others, but my experience has taught me that women really are the stronger sex. If it weren't for testosterone, women would probably rule the planet. During this time I was just angry. And in the midst of all of this, we were in the process of buying a house. The oddest thing happened to further complicate matters is that the person selling the house didn't want to sell it to us. I couldn't figure out why.

Some people thought it was because I had four large Rottweilers, showed them, trained them, bred them, and would have fun with them. A lot of people thought, "Maybe he just doesn't want you moving in that house with those Rottweilers where his mom lived."

But at the time I really couldn't figure it out. So we had to go through a third party which was legal. Our real estate agent was a

God-send. He was a friend of my dad's. I'd gone to school with his kids, and Frank was a wonderful human being. He told us how we could legally go through a third party and buy the house. So we paid full price for the house and we got it. We actually went through one of Mary's sisters and her husband. I was very touched that they did that for us.

Mary and I bought the house the summer that she was gone, and it was just a lot of stress. I was also on the local school board and we were dealing with a teachers' strike, so talk about an interesting time. Doctors say surgeries are stressful, moves are stressful, and I was going through a move from one house to another. I was going through an intensive illness with Mary. So when the school board members were at the negotiating committees, lots of times there'd be some down time, and I would grab a basketball and go down to the gymnasium and shoot baskets. I guess I just put things in perspective. To me, the strike was important, but it certainly wasn't life-threatening.

It was also during the time when I'd go visit Mary that I would be walking out in the parking lot at dusk or late in the afternoon. I honestly wanted somebody to jump out at me. Several times the nurses or other hospital personnel would say, "Be careful," or "Have the security guard escort you out there."

I was thinking, "Oh, no!"

After fifteen years of training in Tae Kwon Do, I wanted somebody to jump out at me. I wanted somebody to try to rob me. I wanted to beat the living shit out of somebody and not get in legal trouble for doing it. I wanted the anger to come out. I wanted a good excuse to try some of the Tae Kwon Do kicks and strikes I knew and to see if I really could snap their arms like we trained for in Tae Kwon Do.

The beast inside of me was growing stronger and more aggressive. It was making me want to do things I normally wouldn't want to do. I really wanted somebody to jump out at me and I just wanted to cut loose on them.

But it never happened. I didn't get rid of the beast, either. It was just strange. I discovered my beast wasn't evil, but it was aggressive and assertive and, at times, violent. It was as if I had a three-way conversation with myself: the beast, my own consciousness, and the little goody-two-shoes side that would always say, "Be peaceful, be merciful, be friendly, and be nice."

The beast was always irritated. He was angry, short-tempered, mad at the world, mad at the fact that Mary was going to die.

And then there was my own consciousness in there with these other two, and it was as though I was half of both sides. I was myself, but yet I had two friends with me. I guess I wasn't an only child after all. I had two friends with me. But it was very difficult. At this time I just didn't know what to do.

Soko von der Mauth, SchH III, ZTP.

CHAPTER SEVEN

Life With the Beast.

I felt sort of strange. I felt like I had multiple personalities now, but yet I wasn't a multiple personality. It was like having different thoughts in my brain or hearing—no, it wasn't really hearing other voices, but it was just like as if you had different thoughts and different characters, sort of like watching a movie. I'd always had fairly consistent behavior in my life, being maybe perhaps a little slightly more aggressive or assertive at times. I wrestled in high school, tried to wrestle in college, boxed for fun in college, and then started taking Tae Kwon Do when I was interviewed to work at the prison.

Working at a maximum security prison definitely changes a person. Being around violence, even if you don't commit the violence, changes you. It makes you much more paranoid, makes you think of things like the crimes that the inmates did which put them in this hell hole of a place.

When I was a teacher at the prison, I would read the inmates' master files to see what made them tick, just like any teacher wants to know of his or her student. The problem was that my students were violent convicted felons in a maximum security prison, and some of the things, hideous, horrible, sick things, I read stuck with me. Some of their crimes, the violence they committed, the inhumanity to their fellow man that they did was just unbelievable, but it would stick with you and it stuck with me. I remembered it, and then all the violence I would see on TV would just magnify it.

I always tried to be a Christian, to keep my faith and to remember that the ultimate goal was to do what God wanted and to get to heaven. But I felt a lot of pressure with Mary's cancer, and it just felt unfair, although I wasn't mad at God, I thought more of the story of Job where Satan was doing this to Mary, putting the cancer in her, and I was mad at Satan. Probably the best way to describe it was that I was disappointed that God had allowed Satan to create bad or painful situations, and God hadn't stopped Satan. I felt more towards God like a child does to a loving parent when the loving parent doesn't let the child do whatever he or she wants.

That's how I felt inside. With the cancer and the pressure from my job, I felt this anger which I call a beast. The best movie or the best way I've ever described it, if somebody can't understand it, was to compare it to the Rocky Balboa movie where Rocky's talking to his brother-in-law. He talks about that beast inside of him when he talks about his wife having died from cancer, and the beast in me was just the part of me that was mad that Mary was going to die.

90

When cancer comes back and when it's metastasized and it has spread from its original organ, it doesn't take a rocket scientist to get on the Internet and look to see that it takes just a few years for the cancer victim to die, that 95% of the people that have cancer that's metastasized would die within five years. It was just unbelievable. Mind numbing may be a better way to describe how reading those statistics felt. There was a smaller percentage that would live seven years or more, however, for the most part within 10 years, almost 100% of cancer victims had died.

I don't mean that to be negative or for those of you reading this book to be without hope or to give up hope, because things have changed a lot since 1999, but that's how I felt at the time. The beast inside of me never seemed to relax. It was just angry and churning. It didn't really want to go out and attack some innocent kid walking down the street or attack some innocent old person driving a car. However, when I would see some jerk in the store talking rudely or disrespectfully to their kid or their spouse, I would just want to smash their face into the counter or pick up a can in the grocery store and throw it at them. It was more of an angry protector that my Beast was, just wanted somebody arrogant or rude to unleash on.

The beast in me, it wasn't evil or cruel, but it was very impatient and at the same time I'd have those thoughts of punching a jerk or breaking their elbow or giving them a Tae Kwon Do kick to their head or their knee or whatever vital organ or body part that popped into my head.

There was another side to me, the gentle side, which had a serene Christian mentality that was also a new side to me. I'd always been a Christian, but this was now a more vocal counterbalance to the beast. I would have some thoughts that would be to one extreme or the other.

"Turn away, walk away, and embrace Christ's teachings."

"If they slap your cheek, turn the other one."

It was curious because I really always tried to embrace Christian principles; however, now I wanted to be much more than I had been. I wanted to be kind, to turn the other cheek, to be peaceful. I wanted to make sure I got to heaven, because Mary was turning into a better Christian. Mary was turning and evolving; changing into a person who was different than the one I married. She wasn't so focused on work or on material things. She'd always been a good Christian person, but now she was much more concerned about people's feelings. It was hard to explain, but I think she realized deep down inside that the end was getting closer, even though the doctors hadn't said that yet.

When we were dating and first married, Mary used to say, "Don't get mad, get even," and she meant it. She could at times be very cold and hard towards people that got on her bad side.

As time went on I was just very, very annoyed, and in me, the beast would get its way more often than not, maybe 90% of the time. From working in a maximum security prison, I was able to get away with that attitude, with that mentality. A lot of people are very aggressive, even the staff. They were very assertive. The staff was very strict at following the law and doing what was legally and morally right, but it's just a very different environment that someone who hasn't worked in would struggle to understand.

This was me, this was what I was turning into, and I was even frustrated at that. My boss at the time told me that I needed to take a leave of absence to be with Mary so he could plan his day; that being there half the time and being gone half the time disrupted and inconvenienced his work planning. This just infuriated me, because I wouldn't be getting paid if I took a leave of absence, and I would use up all of my sick time that I would get paid for.

I didn't know how long Mary was going to be sick and I still needed to make a living. I couldn't go without a pay check, and this fool was trying to force me to do that. I became even madder and more infuriated that this was happening to me.

On top of that, my boss was giving me a hard time, I thought partly because of Mary's illness. He did and said a number of things that were out of line. One of the things he tried to do was make me and another manager work in the prison's Employee Commissary. The Business Office was responsible for the Employee Commissary where the staff can go buy cigarettes and Hostess goodies, potato chips and other snack foods. At that time there were inmates working there who were stealing, and the Employee Commissary wasn't making a profit.

So the warden we had at the time wasn't, in my opinion, the best manager, and I felt that he was also giving me a hard time because of Mary's illness and being gone for the bone marrow transplant. The warden had told my boss that me and the other manager in the Business Office needed to work in the Employee Commissary for a while to see if we could determine who was stealing. We'd take turns doing 12-hour shifts seven days a week. Since we were managers we wouldn't be receiving overtime for this

94

work, and this would stop me from being able to see Mary three of four days a week.

I listened to my Beast this time and enjoyed what I did. To work in a prison food area, or in a commissary, or in one of the kitchens, a person had to pass a food handler's test. It was a questionnaire. The most important focus of this questionnaire was to find out if the individual had HIV or AIDS. As long as an individual didn't and didn't have any communicable diseases, he or she received a food handler's permit.

I told my boss that I wouldn't pass the test for a food handler's permit, and he was stunned.

He said, "What are you saying?"

I replied, "I have HIV."

He looked shocked and said, "No, you don't!"

I responded, "Well, that's what I'm going to tell them on the food handler's questionnaire. My medical records are confidential and since medical records are unavailable to you, you're not going to be able to prove it one way or another. I think I have HIV."

He was pissed. It wasn't until he had taken another job at another prison and I had been promoted into his position that I told this to some of the people that I worked with; that the doctor had made a mistake and that I didn't have HIV, and we all had a good laugh out of it.

Unfortunately, I had some frustrations with different supervisors whom I thought were unfair as a result of Mary being sick. Because of this, occasionally, I probably did or said things that were inappropriate. I remember also telling a different supervisor from a different area with whom I'd had a disagreement that perhaps he should show up at Tae Kwon Do some night. We had one free lesson and we could spar, and it was a veiled threat. He knew exactly what it was, but it wasn't an overt enough threat that I could have gotten in trouble for it.

At the same time, I would have inmates walking around the galleries and in the cell houses always threatening staff and telling staff crazy stuff, such as they were going to kill their families or rape their female loved ones. I was supposed to just ignore it. Occasionally, I would say things back like, "Well, you know what? You better make sure you do kill me, because if you don't, I'm going to kill you and your whole family and your grandma's goldfish."

I was just plain damned angry. In part, I found that my anger and frustrations with Mary's sickness had to just come out. I couldn't hold it in. I had to talk about it and, at times, humor masks pain, and so I would say things that were funny. Sometimes I found that truth presented in a certain way was very funny.

When Mary was diagnosed as terminal, the first part of December 2001, having a position that was probably in some ways equivalent to an Assistant Warden that of being the Chief Fiscal Officer, was a big responsibility, a higher level senior position. Some women that worked at the prison would make me offers that were not appropriate to make to a married man. Some were very subtle, and some were very open,

"Hey, if Mary can't take care of business for ya, come to my house."

Things like that.

I turned them all down, but part of it made me mad. I was incensed, Mary wasn't dead yet, I wasn't a single man yet, but yet, at the same time, I just didn't know how to deal with those offers. I would go home and I would tell Mary, but I also developed an odd sense of humor because of this. Mary and I would talk about these offers of mine. She was glad I told her, however, she felt guilty because she was sick and it was affecting me.

I'd be at a school board meeting where we were discussing something serious and the tension would get high. I'd tell an inappropriate joke to help break the tension. When I was at work, and inmates were talking to other staff or staff were going to have an argument, I would tell a joke to break up the tension. Sometimes it worked, sometimes it didn't, but I had this conflict going inside of me. It changed me and it made me a little different.

I would be frustrated at home, too. With Mary sick and in the hospital for her bone marrow transplant, we hired some cleaning people. In retrospect, they weren't the most reputable, but there weren't a lot of people in a small town of 10,000 that did cleaning. I remember thinking that they were doing some odd things, so I tried to watch them when they were in the house. I believe that they stole some of Tom's money he had in his drawer, but I couldn't prove it. They cleaned the house a few more times, I watched them very closely and then I let them go. I was infuriated that while Mary was in the hospital for an experimental treatment, some scum would steal money from us. I became even more irritated all the while Mary was gone, because I was doing everything and I felt the pressure of being a single parent and a beast developed even more in me.

Since Mary and I had bought the house across the street when Mary was still gone, I also had to clean the bungalow for Mary to return to. I had to paint all of the rooms and remove all the dust in them. The protocol for a bone marrow transplant was very strict. No dust! If any dust got in the lungs, it could cause an infection and kill Mary.

So I had to have all the air ducts in the house cleaned, had to paint the entire house without her there to supervise and when Mary came back, she didn't like the shade. She had previously told me what color and shade to get, which I told the paint store but she didn't like it once she got back. I remember that made me very livid when she complained because I had put all of that hard work into cleaning the house and I felt very unappreciated.

I had been a single parent for four months, doing the best I could with a couple of Rottweilers, a couple of kids, and a stressful job. I was just really frayed around the edges.

I remember one time coming home from seeing Mary. I went to pick up Tom and Sarah at my parents' house, and my mom told me that she and my dad had caught my son, Tom, who was 10 at the time crying in my old bedroom. He was terrified that he was going to be an orphan; that I was going to die in a car wreck, which would leave him without a parent. Tom also, sadly, believed that Mary was going to die. Some of the fourth grade kids had told him that when people get cancer, they die. Tom was beside himself, and we'd been through a stressful time buying the new house.

I had stress from so many different angles of my life to begin with – maintaining a happy marriage, two young children, supporting a family, coping with work issues, and the added responsibility of aging parents.

Now, on top of that, I was dealing with the serious illness; my wife's cancer that had metastasized and was being treated with extreme, experimental, procedures and knowing in the back of my mind that it's probably a death sentence, but nobody really wants to say it.

The stress was unbelievable and, it seemed, even more so for me with my personality split between The Nice Guy and The Beast. I had these different voices in my head telling me what to do, conducting an internal argument, pulling me in many directions. It was just so many different thoughts and ideas that kept popping into my head, which was hard to deal with. I became angry, but yet I still wasn't angry at God. I still had my faith in God that somehow this would be all right, that this would be over.

I don't know how I got through that time, I didn't know what to do, sleeping three hours a night, taking what is now considered an illegal steroid to give me the energy to get through each day. I felt at times like I was going to explode, which would be different than I would feel later after Mary died. But at that time, it felt like there was this thing inside of me that wanted to tear out through my skin, like a monster wanting to bust out of a cage.

This is how I felt, and this is how I think a lot of people feel when they are facing a life-threatening situation, or an extreme situation. So much stress that it's almost unbearable. The point I hope I can get across is that we still have to hold on to our faith; we still have to believe that God has a plan for us.

Me testing to be a Tae Kwon Do Master with Grand Master Kim scoring my reverse spin kick and break.

Me testing to be a Tae Kwon Do Master with Grand Master Kim scoring my push kick.

CHAPTER EIGHT

Mary Comes Home.

Mary got back home after almost four months of being away at Loyola, and she was a different person when she came home. I remember thinking that she wasn't the same person that left here four months ago. I had incorrectly predicted that she would pick up where she was when she left off. With the house, with the kids, with me. The last thing we did before she left to go to Loyola was to make love and try to be positive.

When she came back, she was different. She was distant, irritable, impatient. She wasn't happy with the way I kept the house clean, even though I had hired some house cleaners. She wasn't happy with the way we had painted the house. It was as if she was looking for something to pick a fight over. She was very frustrated, and maybe it was just the frustration of what she'd been through, of being away from home, being away from the kids, being away from me. I don't know. She never really said, but those first few weeks that she was back, she was very irritable, distant, and cold; not only to me but with the kids, as well.

We were in the process of starting to remodel the kitchen in the new house and to paint the inside of it. Mary had told her sister, that she was going to be in charge of the remodeling and not me. That really bothered me. The loss of control in my own house, and that control being taken away by my wife and feeling untrusted by Mary who I had stood by for so long and had put up with so much.

We got into an argument over this. Mary couldn't go in the house we just bought for three months because of the protocol from the bone marrow transplant, and she didn't seem to think that she could trust my judgment on remodeling or painting, and that just infuriated me. Mary and I were the ones who were going to be living there. I told her that she could even peek in the windows and see what was going on, but that her sister wasn't going to tell me what to do.

My relationship with Mary had become distant in some ways, and this was really the first time in our marriage that we had had problems. I think it was just Mary taking control of her life again. She was mad at the situation and taking it out on me. She was mad at not being able to be a mom and a wife for four months. She just was frustrated at everything, and I knew the feeling.

We had been working on the house for several months since her return home, and slowly she started to become more like her old self. My dad and I had painted every room in the house. Mary's brother-in-law, was remodeling the kitchen and building a fence for us. We'd hired a company to re-wire the house, since the wiring was the original 1920s wiring. Mary was spending money like crazy during this time. Her sister called it nesting. Somehow Mary knew that she was going to die, because she mentioned it every so often. She was buying expensive furniture that wasn't extravagant in its looks, but it was extravagant in its durability. She wanted to make as much in the house as permanent and durable as she could, so that when she was gone, Tom and Sarah and I would have a good life.

About this time a new warden took over at the prison. A new governor had taken over in the State, George Ryan, and he had a policy that was to take the prison system back from the control of the inmates according to what I was being told at work. It was a whole different mentality: being firm with the inmates and not allowing them to intimidate the staff. It was a mentality that I fell into very easily.

Within approximately two months of Mary returning from her bone marrow transplant, I started to become closer to the new warden, I thought he was very intelligent and capable. We were working closely together on different projects and seemed to be developing a friendship. He liked my ideas, liked my abilities, and he started talking about promoting me. My current immediate supervisor

105

didn't seem to embrace the new changes that were coming, and he ended up transferring to another prison a year after our new warden came to Pontiac.

In the summer of 2000, I was promoted to the Chief Fiscal Officer position, which at the time we called the Business Administrator. The actual payroll title was Public Service Administrator, which was the second highest title the State of Illinois had in Corrections, and I enjoyed the work. I had a different mentality than the old Chief Fiscal Officer. On things that he couldn't control, he would just say, "I'm going to wash my hands of it and not worry about it," and he would just let things happen however they happened.

Inaction or the wrong actions on his part caused a department of 40 people to have probably 20-30 grievances a month through the union. My old boss also had a habit of not sticking to what he said. I don't know if it was intentionally or unintentionally, but we heard the phrase lots of times, "Prove I said that."

So when I took over there I certainly felt some stress and worry, but I thought, "If I'm proactive and I get in there and I'm assertive and grab the bull by the horns, I could do a pretty good job."

When I left as the Business Administrator a little over four years later, we had had two audits by the Auditor General's Office from the State, and we had perfect audits, so I think I did do a pretty good job. I had been given the highest overall rating from two different wardens that I could get on my performance evaluations while in that position by the time I took the early retirement buy-out.

This now leads to something that Mary and I had discussed years before. She was a little frustrated that I hadn't tried to be promoted and that I hadn't sought a higher job title with more money, but at the time I really didn't want to. Tom was younger, then we had Sarah, and Mary had cancer. I just wanted to enjoy life.

Now that she had had the cancer the second time and had just got done with the bone marrow transplant, my new warden had said, "You know, the odds are Mary will probably die, and you're going to need more money."

So I put on my big-boy pants, and I grew up and I tried to become more responsible.

The funny thing was that I seemed to be doing a good job. I reported directly to the warden now, and he wanted to promote me even more. I'm not saying this to pat myself on the back. I'm saying this to get to a point, because when I went home and told Mary, she was upset. She realized that in my current position I had to do some socializing, go out for drinks after work sometimes and do things that

107

took away from our home life. My job responsibilities required me at times to go into work on weekends and on holidays. I still remember having to go in one Christmas Eve, because supplies weren't delivered in order to give the inmates their "Christmas lump", as we called it. It was an assortment of toiletries and candies that they could buy in the commissary, but we gave it out free at Christmas time.

Mary had not thought ahead and realized this, I think. She thought I could just do my job and still have the same amount of time at home. When I told her that I had been offered a chance to move into a superintendent's spot for a few months and then be moved into the Assistant Warden of Programs job, since I was a teacher and understood the programs that we tried to do for the inmates, she broke down crying. I still remember. It was in the kitchen, and she said, "Please don't do it, please."

I think she knew I wanted to take the position, that I'd like it. I felt very guilty at the time and I still do looking back, but I enjoyed her crying. I enjoyed her begging me not to take a promotion, because I felt vindication knowing that she had realized she was wrong when she had belittled me for not getting promoted earlier in my career.

That still bothers me to this day, and I don't know for sure why I did feel so gleeful, in a way, that she was crying. It was vindictive, and I was gleeful. I was thinking, "See I told ya. You're not going to like this." It still bothers me that I felt good watching her cry and I wish I hadn't felt that way, but that Beast inside of me enjoyed it.

Right before I got my promotion, we moved into our new house across the street, the prairie style house as we called it. One of the things that I noticed about Mary after we moved in was that work wasn't important to her. She wanted to stay in this beautiful house we had and make it more of a home. She wanted to be around the kids and me. I also think that's why she didn't want me to be promoted higher than the Chief Fiscal Officer.

During this same time, Mary was becoming good friends with our new housekeeper, Denise, who we ended up calling Hazel. Denise became a close family friend and still is. As Mary evolved into more of a homebody, she did not feel that work and money were as important as they once were. She seemed to nest, as we called it, and to build something that would last Tom, Sarah and myself, until Tom and Sarah went off to college.

My job was good, I was enjoying it. I was going in a different direction at work than the previous Chief Fiscal Officers who had that job before me. I was more of a proactive type of person. The grievances in the office dropped. I treated everyone like I wanted to

109

be treated, because I realized that with Mary's illness, life is short. Somebody could be here today and gone tomorrow, and really, what do we all want? I wanted to be liked, I wanted to be treated fairly, and that's what everybody wants.

For a while the beast inside of me was happy. I was assertive. I was doing the right things. I was getting the anger out, because I was making changes and doing things, accomplishing things that I thought were important. The gentle side of me was happy, too, because I was being fair to people. The grievances in my office dropped to maybe one to two every few months, and those few grievances I had were beyond my control.

I would do things, too, at work that was different than some of my previous bosses in the Business Office did. Typically, the budget people, the money people, would only do something if the rules say they could. I looked at it a different way. If the rules said I couldn't do it, I wouldn't do it. However, if the rules didn't mention it, I figured I could do it, and so did my Warden and Deputy Director. I was able to impress the Warden and the Deputy Director, my bosses on the operations side, and I felt good. I went to various meetings. I shared my ideas. It was probably the best time of my life professionally.

At the same time, I realized that Mary's health was deteriorating. When she came back from the bone marrow transplant, her cancer count was right around 30; a little bit lower once or twice in the high 20s, but it had started to slowly creep up. She came home in September of 1999 and by August or September of 2000, a few months after I had gotten promoted, her cancer count had started to creep up into the 50's and 60's.

The oncologist was nervous. He started ordering some scans and some x-rays, but they revealed nothing new. So her doctor simply monitored her over the next few months, but we knew what was happening, and I took my frustrations in life out at work. I worked a lot. I tried hard. I ended up working anywhere from 50-60 hours a week. It was a good escape for me.

It was at this time that I started my first drug of choice, adrenaline, when I would feel very angry or feel the walls closing in on me and the thought of Mary dying weighed heavily on me. I somehow discovered that if I would get an adrenaline rush when I had these negative feelings, I would become happy and the negative feelings would disappear for a time. To get my rush I would go to the cell houses and make tours like I had always done, but I would walk down the inmate gallery or other areas where inmates were unconfined, and

I hadn't done that before. It was a self-test, to put myself in a dangerous situation, get my rush and challenge myself, seeing if I could do risky and foolish things without being assaulted by the inmates.

There were some very bad people in the Pontiac Correctional Center. We not only had the typical felons who were convicted of murder and assault, but we also had a Death Row and a Mental Health Unit where some super maximum security inmates were housed that had mental issues.

My Beast was gaining control over my actions and that wasn't the smartest thing I could have chosen to do.

Mary right before the bone marrow transplant, April 1999.

112

CHAPTER NINE

Failure!

Mary's bone marrow transplant failed. The cancer count started going up in the summer of 2000 and just slowly crept up through the fall. Dr. Jeong wanted to see what was going on. He did some scans and x-rays, and they didn't show any cancer. He even did PET scan that didn't show anything. A PET scan's a little bit different than an MRI or an X-ray. It's a scan that shows hot spots in the body. From what was explained to us, the hot spots are typically where the cancer is, because those cells move faster. It's similar to what is seen on TV with those thermal imaging goggles or scopes that the police use to look through walls of houses and see people moving based on their heat signatures.

The PET scan didn't show anything. However, throughout the fall, Mary's cancer count kept going up, and finally Dr. Jeong said in November that he was going to just start Mary back on chemo because we knew something was going on.

The cancer was growing, the cancer count was going up. The cancer count was explained to us fairly simply, so that helped Mary and me understand. All the cells in the human body eat food and excrete waste. Cancer cells do the same thing: they eat the food, they poop out waste. However, their waste product, their "poop" so to speak, changes the chemical balance of the blood. When a blood test is done for specific types of cancer, ours being breast cancer, the cancer count is determined on basically how much cancer poop is in the blood.

And so Mary's cancer count was going up. For a normal person, a normal woman, the cancer count is anywhere between 0-30. After the bone marrow transplant, Mary's was bouncing in the high 20s and low 30s, but it began creeping up into the 40s and 50s, but yet nothing was showing up on the PET scan. Finally, Dr. Jeong had us start on the chemo.

The cancer count kept going up. We couldn't understand it. Both of us were scared. We didn't know what to do. What was causing the rise in the count. This caused a lot more stress. I just wanted to ask God in person, "Why was this happening? How come this was happening to us, to me?"

Really, it started becoming an issue with me. Yeah, Mary was my wife, I loved her, I didn't want this to happen. Somehow, as time went on and the stress built up, I seemed to focus more on what was happening to me, because it was my wife, it was affecting my life.

Looking back, I recognize that it was selfish to think that way, but at the time, that's just how I thought.

We realized that the cancer count increase and Mary's additional chemo was a death sentence. Nobody said it, but we understood that the bone marrow transplant hadn't worked. The black cloud was over us again. We were very anxious and depressed, apprehensive and nervous, and we wondered what was going to happen next.

Around the end of November, one of the PET scans showed some hot spots on Mary's lungs again. That's where they had been initially, that's where they come back. During the summer of 2000, Mary was becoming more like her old self, even though the cancer count was sneaking up. She was relaxed and she wasn't as cold or as distant. Mary and I talked a lot more. We did more together. I got promoted and we were enjoying talking about work a lot. We seemed to have fun doing things together again. When the Christmas party for work came around, we really had a good time. That was the last truly wonderful outing that we had together before we knew the cancer was officially back.

The beast was getting the worst of me at times, because I was angry at what was happening to Mary. The cancer count was going up and we couldn't find where the cancer was growing.

I didn't think the doctor was telling us everything that he knew. He wasn't giving us the hard facts. We would ask him hard questions, "If the cancer is back, how much time?"

Time was our big issue because we had young children. He didn't want to tell us, but we wanted to know. Looking back, we must have realized that the doctor honestly didn't know, but it was very frustrating to us, especially me. I started having thoughts of just smashing things: the furniture, objects, turning file cabinets over at work when I'd get mad. It was just very disheartening!

As 2000 turned into 2001 and Mary was doing chemo, I started doing a lot more things alone and take on more of the family duties. If Mary was sick, I had to do activities with the kids. I had to do more shopping. I had to pick up the pace as far as the household things went. I was doing more at work, having more responsibility, and at the same time I was doing more at home. I was getting very discouraged, plus I was feeling very alone, and it was getting worse with time.

In looking back over the last 10 years, that was really when my anger started to escalate. It just kept getting worse over the next 10 years.

As I did more and more things alone, I began to feel fairly uncomfortable. Before this period, Mary would do things with me one time and then maybe not the next or she'd do two things with me, then maybe none. It was intermittent. But now, it was getting to be the other way around. I would do two, three, four things by myself where we should've been a couple, and she wasn't there. Because lots of times she had no energy or she was nauseated. I felt especially awkward at her niece's graduation, because that was really the first time I did a family function on Mary's side of the family without Mary. They were all very nice and kind to me, but it was just strange without Mary.

As the summer of 2001 got here, Mary was very sick from the chemo. Her cancer kept growing and the chemo didn't really stop it, so now the cancer was showing up on scans and x-rays, and that wasn't good at all. We were definitely becoming more and more scared every time we went to the doctor. And I was becoming angrier, antagonistic, belligerent, and resentful. I had thoughts of beating people who pissed me off. I even wanted to punch friends who made me mad. I wasn't just thinking of punching them, I was thinking of doing the Tae Kwon Do moves I had learned and hurting them. I just was disturbed. I wanted to be good because I knew Mary was going to die, and I wanted to be good so I could go to heaven and see everybody that I'd loved that had died. So it was an internal struggle. I was very aggravated, and I didn't know what to do, much less how to channel these negative feelings and emotions.

For the most part though, work was good. It was rewarding. I had a lot of fun there and friends to help me cope. It was a very challenging and rewarding career for me. I was friends with my boss, the warden, with a lot of upper management, and there was a close camaraderie. We were a team. It was a maximum security prison and we were working together, and that camaraderie helped me. Many times my co-workers would come to the house and say, "Let's go have a beer," or they would take me out after work. Even during work hours the warden would tell us that we were going to have a lunch meeting. Yes, we'd go to a restaurant, but to get away from the workplace and simply talk about work - nothing formal. It helped me a lot.

I was enjoying work because I was pushing the limits. I was doing things that hadn't been done before. I was changing the way things had been done, just because it'd been done that way. I questioned, "Why do we do it that way?" When nobody could give me a valid reason why not to do something or state the accounting rules that prohibited it, I did it. The warden and the deputy director, they were happy with me. They liked what I did.

I had changed some things around with the way we sold pop and snacks to the employees. We were making money hand over fist. We were able to have parties. In fact, with the money we made, we had a carnival one year with our prison and the other prison that was close to us, a maximum security prison at Dwight for women. We had the staff party for both prisons. I was making souvenirs and selling them as mementos at our Employee Commissary. A number of people came in to the commissary, different dignitaries or higher-ups from other prisons, and even regular staff from other prisons. They thought it was cool that they could buy a sweatshirt that said "Pontiac Correctional Center" or a tee shirt that said the "Illinois Department of Corrections." I had a lot of fun. Everybody seemed to enjoy it.

When I went to meetings, I structured my reports similarly to a teacher's lesson plan. I included colored graphs. That way, the non-business people could understand what I was talking about. My life at work was really good. I was enjoying it, having fun, and able to cope with my duties and responsibilities. I always made sure I had the Deputy Director's favorite soda in the Warden's office refrigerator, and the Deputy Director would always tell me I was the best Business Administrator in the Department.

The chemo wasn't working for Mary, and that bothered us. We were scared. But there was even more to be scared of. There were side effects from the chemo that were life-threatening. Mary's potassium was going dangerously low, as well as her blood counts. This necessitated more trips to the hospital for transfusions of blood or of potassium. The cancer was still growing even though she was taking chemo. Knowing this worked on us. We knew deep down inside that death was coming like a little tick, tick, tick of a clock or the slow scratch of fingernails across a chalkboard.

In the beginning of December, 2001, Dr. Jeong told us that Mary was going to die. He said she was terminal. There was nothing more he could do but try to slow it down. His analogy at the time was, "This cancer's like a freight train and really all we can do is throw rocks at it."

He wanted us to tell the kids. Mary struggled to keep control of her emotions. I wanted to vomit. It was like somebody had kicked me in the nuts. Mary asked if she could wait until after Christmas, and Dr. Jeong said it was okay, but not too long.

When he said, "not too long," my ears started ringing. I couldn't believe it. Now what did that mean? Was she going to die soon? With a barrage of questions from us, Dr. Jeong just said he didn't know. He told us that there would be a good chance she could live for about six years. But it didn't make sense to me. If she could live for six years, why did we have to hurry up and tell the kids right after Christmas?

When we went home, I was just dumbfounded. I wandered around the house, just aimlessly wandered around the house. I was totally crushed and devastated. I couldn't believe this. This lasted for several days, if not weeks. In fact, I was even crying at work with friends. I'd go in different offices to visit with my friends and tell them what the doctor had said, and I would cry. I would try to tell them without crying, but it would end up being a cry fest. Most of the time they would cry with me. We would joke later about all us tough guys crying together.

I started drinking more. I took more risks at work. I wanted that adrenaline rush. I wanted to forget what was going on. I didn't want to deal with reality. I was very lost. I was very angry. A close friend of mine by the name of Emily was sitting in my office one day talking to me. She was a counselor who was trying to help and be very sweet, and I said, "People are just pissing me off. I don't know why they're pissing me off."

She replied, "Think about it, Mike. Nobody's really trying to piss you off. You're like a loose cannon going to explode, and nobody wants you to explode on them."

She added, "My God, you're like a giant. You're what, 6'8"?"

I commented, "No, I'm 6'4"." Some of my staff had told me that I scared the "shit out of them" when I was upset or in a bad mood. They knew what was going on in my life and the stress I was under and they all seemed to wait for the big explosion from my office.

But at the same time I realized that everybody could see that I was like this loose cannon going to explode.

My friends were great. They would get me to hang with them after work, and I enjoyed this. I wanted to avoid home. For some reason, I didn't want to go home. If I went home, it meant the day was over. Not that I wanted to avoid Mary or the kids, I didn't want the day to be over. I was successful and in control at work. I wanted to slow down time. I wanted time to stop, because I knew as time went on,

Mary was going to die. I also became closer to my dad at this time. I really leaned on him. He was my rock. He was my helper.

Mary at this time seemed resigned to the death sentence after the initial shock wore off, and she expected it. She knew it was going to come. She talked about it. She said she knew from the beginning when she first got cancer that it was going to get her. She seemed to kick the nesting mode into high gear, buying new furniture and redoing the house a little bit, buying different cooking utensils, pots, pans, mixers, expensive, high-end, long-lasting things.

She also began in earnest spoiling the kids. For Tom's 13th birthday, she bought a fancy Dale Earnhardt Monte Carlo. Now let me tell you about this. Mary was normally a pretty good bargain hunter, but she liked this car. She asked me about it, but she was pretty much in charge. She asked Tom if he'd rather have a red Monte Carlo or the black one with the Dale Earnhardt emblems. Tom wanted the black one. He liked it.

So when Tom was 13, Mary bought this car. She was going to drive it until she died and then we could park it until Tom turned 16. He'd then have the car that his mom got just for him. It was all sort of funny. Because when I was dating Mary I would buy her flowers from time to time just to be nice and let her know I cared. After we were engaged she told me to stop buying her flowers and save the money to put on her china pattern. Now she buys a 13-year-old kid a new car! It was so unlike the Mary I met and fell in love with.

One day, Mary wanted to go out to the Dairy Queen, and when we were there, she wanted to drive by the car dealership. Her sister was getting a different used car, and she wanted to be nosey and see what was going on, what kind of car it was.

As we were driving through the car dealer's, she pointed out a car and said, "I've always liked those. Those are nice-looking. What kind of car is it again?"

"It's a Monte Carlo, Mary."

She responded, "Yeah, I've always liked those."

I commented, "Well, you know what? If you want one, go get one, because there really is no tomorrow for you," not really expecting her to do that.

So what did she do? She did exactly that. She went out the next day and traded in my three-year-old pickup truck that I loved on a Monte Carlo. That normally wasn't like her, but she was spoiling the kids. I was given Mary's SUV to drive after she traded my truck, but that was OK, she had a cool car and it made her happy.

Mary was also buying new things for Sarah. Sarah liked clothes. That seemed to be Mary's enjoyment, going shopping with Sarah, and buying Sarah clothes. Mary also did something quite unlike her in the past. She started buying extras for herself, including a lot of jewelry. With our friend, Patty, Mary would get on the Internet and look at different jewelry sites and with Patty's encouragement, Mary would buy some.

At that point, Mary had also returned to telling me what to do when she was gone. I didn't want to hear that, and I think that was part of the reason I wanted to drink more and avoid the house. I didn't want to think about it. She started talking about her feelings of me being with another woman. She was very open. She didn't want me to be alone. She didn't want me to suffer. She wanted me to find somebody, because she knew I needed somebody. As much as we men talk about being tough and able to do everything a woman can, let me tell ya, we're a train wreck when we live by ourselves.

Because she knew this, Mary encouraged me to find another woman. A new partner when she was gone, but at the same time, she said it made her feel funny. She, at one time in her life, had hoped that she'd be the only woman I was ever with. Being a Christian trying to embrace God's teaching, I was a virgin when I met

Mary, a 22-year-old virgin. It wasn't quite as bad as the movie, *40-year-old Virgin*, but it was almost as funny.

Mary wanted to help me move on after she died. We talked a lot about that, what specifically to do and how to find another wife. At the same time, when she was feeling good, she seemed to want to have more sex. I didn't mind that.

I also found out from the kids that when I wasn't home, if she thought she was alone and they were watching TV, they would hear her crying or they would peek around the corner and see her crying.

When we did tell Tom that Mary was going to die, he took it hard but he was fairly stoic. His eyes got teary and watery and red, and he told us that he knew that eventually she'd die because she had cancer.

We tried to tell Sarah, but Sarah just didn't understand or wouldn't listen, or maybe she was smarter than we realized, she would change the subject and run, because she didn't want to hear it.

One day after Mary had been shopping with some friends and Sarah was along, she brought up the subject of her death with Sarah in the car. Sarah couldn't get away from it. I still remember when the car pulled in the driveway that day, I heard the doors open and a terrible, terrible scream, a crying scream, and then a door slammed.

Little feet were just running up the sidewalk into the door, a bang to the door. She opened it, she pushed on it, she didn't shut it, and she was screaming looking for me. Screaming bloody murder and crying - the type of cry that every parent cringes when they hear it, because they know their child has been hurt and something terrible has happened to them.

Sarah didn't have anything physically wrong. She wasn't bleeding, she didn't have a broken bone, but her heart was crushed. She ran in to me, hugging me, tears rolling down her face screaming and crying that, "Mommy's going to die. Mommy's going to die," just hugging me, tighter than she'd hugged me for a long, long time. And I didn't know what to do.

It was hard for me to deal with everything. Even though I liked my job, the responsibility of budgeting $55,000,000 and supervising a staff of 40 people, balancing work and family was a lot of pressure, a lot responsibility. It wasn't fair that Mary should have a young family and face a death sentence.

In some ways, I felt like I was the last priority in Mary's life. She was more worried about how the kids felt. She was worried about how her parents felt. She was worried about how her sisters felt. In retrospect, I realize she was trying to balance everybody that she loved and help them deal with her terminal illness.

But to me, being her husband, I felt like I was last on the list, and I pulled away from Mary. I regret this now, and I have a lot of guilt, but I pulled away emotionally. Physically I was there, I was at the house, but emotionally I pulled away. I tried to numb myself.

I was also very perturbed with Dr. Jeong. I felt like he was giving us two different stories. He would try to paint a rosier picture, a more hopeful picture for us.

One of the guys I worked with had a wife who was a nurse at the hospital where Mary usually went. I would hear stories of what the doctor said behind closed doors or what the nurses discussed with each other. Doctors are smart and they know a lot, and so do nurses. They're the ones in there helping the patients. The doctors see them and leave. The nurses are there for 12-hour shifts. They know what the patients go through. They know what they look like. They know when they die. They know when the signs are coming, and it had to be hard on them. I heard one version of Mary's current status from the nurses, and I would push to get the answers, and then we heard another story from Dr. Jeong. It was just exasperating.

128

I ended up getting some counseling because I was so angry all the time. I was afraid I would punch someone at work. Luckily, we had a lot of counselors at work with whom I would talk. We had some ministers at the prison, too, which I would talk to, and I even went to a shrink at the local hospital.

Tom and Sarah with Cella.

CHAPTER 10

My Struggles.

I had seen a shrink right after Mary was diagnosed as terminal. It was very stressful seeing a shrink, because people that saw shrinks were crazy, or so I thought and, although I had a couple of voices in my head, I had my beast and my serene Christian voice, as I call it. But I was unable to cope with Mary's diagnosis alone and without professional support. I felt like a pinball bouncing around at times.

Mary was taking the chemo. It was right before Christmas 2001 that Dr. Jeong told us that Mary was terminal, and since I was the Business Administrator, the Chief Fiscal Officer, I had to go to the Christmas party, the prison Christmas party. I was just expected to go to it as an upper level manager. I went without Mary. She'd been taking chemo and really couldn't be exposed to people who were sick or to take a chance of eating something that wasn't clean, that didn't meet the chemo protocol.

I drove with two friends, John and Mike. John's wife Patty and Mike's the girlfriend were already at the party location helping set up the party. As I rode with my two close friends, we talked about Mary dying. I told them of some of my fears and worries, and I was

130

surprised when they both started talking about the women they knew who wanted to date me. I was taken off guard. I was flabbergasted. Women were talking about wanting to date me? For God's sakes, I hadn't dated for years. I'd been married for years. I'd been married almost 20 years, so I was stunned. Hell, it scared me!

It suddenly sank in, "Oh, my God! I may go back in the dating world."

It was one thing to talk about with Mary, but now other people knew about the fact that Mary was dying. That I might be on the market again and they were talking about it.

At the time, dating other women was really the farthest thing from my mind. Somehow I wanted to make Mary better. I didn't know what to do. Hell, I struggled with dating when I was young. What do I do when I'm in my forties and I start dating again?

As we got to the party, it was very awkward without Mary. Some of our mutual friends who were females seemed to be very motherly to me, nothing inappropriate, but it was very awkward. I missed Mary. I felt out of place. That lonely feeling was creeping in, just as the cold on a winter day does when one is outside too long. As the party went on, I thought about the conversation on the way to the party. I looked around the room at the single women wondering who had said they would like to date me. I was glad I didn't know.

However, as time went on over the next couple of months, I did start getting offers from females with whom I worked with for their companionship. Some were very open about it, some were very subtle. One very attractive woman blatantly propositioned me, telling me she understood men had needs and that while she liked Mary, she understood that I had needs and she'd be very discreet. I turned her down.

Although it was very strange, I was trying to be decent but not sound flirty or give the impression that I would change my mind. At the same time I wished I would've taken her up on it, because she was very attractive.

It was a struggle, like that old joke that says, "You're going to hate yourself in the morning."

Well, I hated myself right then. But I knew I couldn't. I had to be honorable. If I cheated on Mary, it wouldn't be honorable. In my mind, my beast and my Christian side were both agreeing. Only a piece of shit would cheat on his sick, dying wife, and I wasn't going to do that. I still had my faith. I was struggling to keep my faith, and I knew I couldn't cheat on Mary.

I had a few more offers. Some were subtle, some were as simple as bringing in baked goods, single women bringing in baked goods, brownies, cookies. Of course with that, I played dumb and ate them. I know, it's one thing to turn down sex with women who aren't your wife, but if they're being a little bit subtle in bringing their baked goods while they flirt with you, you know what? I can play dumb and eat the brownies and the cookies. Brownies and chocolate chip cookies are my weakness. Good thing none of those women came up to me naked and covered in brownies or cookies. Temptation may have won out.

The other strange thing that happened to me in my struggles is that I started to look at every woman as a possible replacement for Mary. In my mind, I had a mental checklist. Would they be good with Tom and Sarah? Would they like Rottweilers? Would they let me do my Tae Kwon Do? What kind of a housekeeper were they? Were they tall, were they short, and what did I want? Did I want more kids? I had when Mary was first diagnosed. Did I still? I wasn't sure, maybe with the right woman. It wasn't that I was going to cheat, and at times I felt very guilty for thinking about this. But every woman had a checklist. The funny thing was sooner or later, there was a deal-breaker on that checklist, and in my mind I thought, "Nope, take them

133

off the list." I felt scared, I felt lost and panicky and, at times, I even felt trapped. What was I going to do? I couldn't raise Tom and Sarah by myself. I didn't feel that I had the skills to raise Tom and Sarah to be good, decent, Christian people. It was too hard of a job for me to do alone. I couldn't keep a house going. I realized that I can run a department with 40 people in it and 50 some million dollars, but I couldn't run a household. My old fear of being alone was a predator in my mind, and that fear stalked me not only when I was awake but also in my sleep. This fear of being alone had its origin in my being an only child and doing work alone, without anyone to help me. I don't still feel this way now, but at that time before I realized that I had to do it, and that I could do it, I felt this overwhelming fear of being a single parent.

It was hard to focus at work. I wandered around the prison more. I took risks walking in places I shouldn't, going down galleries where there were too many loose inmates and the tower guards weren't watching. I walked down Death Row, walked through some of the yards when the inmates were in them and when the high-security inmates were in their exercise pods as we called them, which looked like dog runs. I would get into verbal sparring matches with the inmates. I needed the high I got from the adrenalin. I had to avoid reality if I could.

I wished it was just over, too. I wished Mary would die, and I felt very guilty about that. There were times I would just pray to God, "Either heal Mary or take her. I can't deal with this limbo land."

When I went to the shrink I told him that, and he told me that was normal. I argued with him.

So he said, "I want you to take a minute, close your eyes, and pretend that God walked in the room. You get to ask God one request and He will grant it. So take a minute and think about it."

At the end of that minute he said, "Open your eyes and tell me what it would be," and I said without missing a beat that I'd want Mary to be healthy and whole again, never have had the cancer and to have all her body parts and no scars and no funny looks or no loss of hair.

He responded, "But since that can't be, it's normal for you to just want it to be over."

He told me that I was grieving her death now even though she wasn't dead yet. He said that I knew her death was coming and that I had started the mourning process. It was a normal reaction.

He went on to tell me that I would heal quicker after she died than the kids would. To them, if she was alive in the morning when they woke up their day was fine. The day that they wake up and she is gone they would start their mourning process, which I had already begun.

In the long run, I found out that men really aren't made the same way that women are. If a man finds a sick puppy on the street, he'll take it to the vet, he'll tell the vet to fix it, and he'll pay the money to have the vet fix it. But if the vet says that there's really not much chance, most men will just leave the puppy there and tell the vet to put it down. Women, on the other hand, would take the puppy home and try to nurse it back to health. Men truly are from Mars and women are from Venus, and this example is one of those areas.

I began drinking more, almost every day. Sometimes just a little bit, sometimes enough to get a good buzz. The days at work were struggles. I enjoyed my work. I enjoyed what I did, if I could keep my mind off Mary. I had a secretary at the time. She was temporarily assigned in there. A very young, fun, entertaining person named Jenny, and we were friends. She kept things at work fun, a silly fun that youth can find in everything, even in a maximum security prison.

I went to some of the other offices. We had an Audit Office where some friends worked, and I would go there and hang out. We had lunch together, mostly talked about work, but it was just being with people that I could trust that helped me. One of the guys I supervised had a wife who was one of the nurses at the hospital where Mary always went. I could find out things through him, and that helped.

I also talked with the chaplains at work, as well as the counselors, and that helped, too. One of the guys I talked to had recently dealt with the death of his wife, and he was a great help. He could relate to what I was going through.

So as time went on, my friend and boss retired, went out of state to another prison, and we got another warden. He was nice, he liked me and he liked my work, but we weren't really friends.

Things stayed about the same for the next two years. Mary was in and out of the hospital, and she had some surgeries, nothing major. The doctors would find a lump growing on her lungs, and they would go in and take it out, but for the most part, the cancer was just spreading out very thinly around her lungs, on her ribs and her chest wall. There were no tumor masses, but it was just all over. When they would find a tumor mass, they'd go in and they'd get it. Mary had over six surgeries in a four-year period.

It drained me, I was tired of worrying, tired of working full time and being a care giver, I was tired of not knowing when Mary was going to die and expecting her to die with every surgery. Mary was also tired and emotionally drained. She was distant to both Tom and Sarah along with me. Tom just took all this in stride, but Sarah started to become clingy with my dad who watched Sarah when Mary and I were at work or the hospital.

Her last surgery was in May of 2004, and she almost didn't make it. I was very scared, hiding in her room and not in the surgery waiting room where there was a crowd of people waiting on the several surgeries that the hospital was performing that morning. I was up in Mary's hospital room playing on my computer. I didn't want to know what was going on, didn't want to talk to anybody, I just wanted to be alone. I knew about what time she was supposed to be done, and it was around that time the doctor came up and talked to me. He told me that if he knew her lungs were in as bad a shape as they were, he would not have operated, because he almost lost her. He told me that her lungs were very bad and even the lung tissue that didn't have cancer on it was red and inflamed from the cancer being so close by.

He let me know when she'd be out of recovery, so around that time I went down, but she was not there yet. I waited for over an hour and then I started asking questions. One nurse would tell me one thing, and another nurse would tell me something different.

About two and a half to three hours after Mary was supposed to be out of recovery, I started getting very frustrated. I called the surgeon, and he told me to call the hospital administrator, which I did. The administrator said he'd have somebody look into it, and before long I had some head nurse talking to me. I could tell she was just giving me a line of bullshit.

I became so frustrated with the round and round circles. I wanted to see my wife. They wouldn't let me. I felt like I was losing self-control; my beast was taking over. I kept thinking that this woman didn't know what she's doing, that she's just making me madder, and before long, my eyes were literally seeing things blurry, my ears were ringing, I felt lightheaded, and the only thought I had was to smash this woman's face. I thought of different ways to smash it. I thought of different things to smash it into. I thought about trying to literally rip her arms out and what they would look like if I popped them out of the socket.

I'd been taking Tae Kwon Do for a long time, and I truly wanted to try different techniques to break her arms. I never learned the tournament style of Tae Kwon Do fighting or sparring. I knew it, but what I concentrated on was the traditional Tae Kwon Do. The Tae Kwon Do that Master Kim had taught when he was in the Korean Army, how to fight somebody and survive. That's what I wanted to learn when I was at the prison working, and that's what I was thinking about now. What if I hit here? What if I punch there? What if I twisted and held under the arm and kicked at this spot or kicked a leg at that spot? Would I truly shatter the bone, would I shatter the knee?

I had broken a 2 x 4 one time when I was testing for a belt. Master Kim said he'd never seen anybody break a 2 x 4. Maybe it was just the right condition of the wood, maybe I had hit it just at the right spot, but I had a lot of confidence that I could break this woman's bones, and I wanted to. I held on to the thought that the last thing my children needed was to have their dad in jail because he beat up a nurse.

Mary had almost died during the surgery, her blood pressure dropped and the surgeon couldn't get Mary stabilized for a few

140

minutes and her heart was beating at over 200 beats per minute. This had happened to her before in a previous surgery and it happened this time also. While Mary was in recovery, her heart beat was irregular and her blood pressure was all over the charts for a few hours.

I was working out a lot. I did a lot of cardio at the time, a lot of Tae Kwon Do to try to control myself, to try to feel better. Tae Kwon Do taught me balance and that's what I needed right now at this moment in time.

Drinking didn't seem to work and I was working out. I started going to Tae Kwon Do more, and I began to do more cardio workouts along with the Tae Kwon Do. I also added to my duties what they called "drug drops" at work. As the manager who was called in to supervise the drug testing of employees to make sure they weren't using drugs, that really frustrated me. I didn't want to do that particular task. I wanted to be home at night with my wife and my kids. I was scared that I would leave and Mary would die and the kids would find her.

One time when I left for about three hours, Mary got a blood clot in her neck, and she literally blew up like the Michelin Man or the Pillsbury Doughboy. She had trouble walking sometimes and

141

breathing, and depending on what chemo she'd had or if she'd had surgery, she would be gray and green and yellow or pink. She would sleep all over the house. She'd sleep in our bed for an hour and then she'd go to the recliner, then she'd go to the couch, then she'd go to the other recliner, then she'd go to a regular chair. We never knew where we'd find her sleeping. It was like a game of "Where's Waldo!!" She couldn't get comfortable. She wanted to find someplace that would allow her to sleep and breathe and be comfortable. When I would find her sleeping in other parts of the house, I would walk up to her to see if she was still alive. I was afraid that I would find her dead some day.

But after her surgery in May, I was very worried about her. I tried to get work done in the morning and then use some of my sick time to go home in the afternoon. I did that for a couple months, and then all of a sudden, the Warden started giving me a hard time. I'd heard different stories that pressure was coming from his boss, the new Deputy Director. I also heard that criticism was coming from the union because I was a manager, and I was getting different treatment than union people. I don't know what was true. I know I was frustrated. I had turned in a note from the doctor which recommended that I take this time off in the afternoons to help Mary recover from her surgery, but it wasn't on the right type of letterhead. I turned in some other paperwork and it wasn't quite right. So I was very infuriated.

I asked one of the ladies who worked for me in the Insurance Department to bring me Mary's whole file. I took her file and started highlighting all the information about her breathing problems, all the reports about her cancer, all the diagnoses about her heart being in bad shape from the chemo. I took that into the Warden's secretary. I gave it to her and said, "Here's the documentation. Here's the proof of why I need to be home. Give it to the Warden."

It wasn't long until I received an email from the Warden, somewhat sarcastic, somewhat smart-assed, directing me that I needed a note from the doctor to the Warden listing specific recommendations for me related to being with Mary.

I snapped. I started cussing. I got up from my desk. Luckily, one of the ladies who worked for me, a very, very sweet lady by the name of Colleen, asked me what was wrong.

I replied that I was going to go beat the shit out of the Warden. She stood in front of the door and she stopped me. She made me think.

She said, "Mary doesn't need this, your kids don't need this. Don't get fired. An early retirement package is coming and you can get out of here."

She talked me out of it. I knew right then that I sincerely would've walked into the Warden's office and beaten the shit out of him. Not a good thing to do when he's your boss, not a good thing to do period.

In reality, it probably would've been a felony and I would've lost my retirement. I would've been fired, disgraced, and an embarrassment to my family, but at the time I didn't care.

So I did start looking at the early retirement. The governor at the time was talking about closing the prison. Managers weren't getting pay raises. Managers supposedly weren't going to be able to be transferred if the prison closed. I didn't know what to do. More stress, more pressure, just what I needed.

I ended up taking an early retirement. It was actually an early retirement buyout. So I left on September 1, 2004, a job I loved, a job that was my dream job, because I thought that I needed to get away from the stress and take care of my wife and children.

CHAPTER 11

Breaking Point.

On September 1, 2004, I took the early retirement that the State was offering. I left the job that was probably the pinnacle of my career and decided to go back to teaching. Mary had told me it was up to me to do what I thought was right. My dad wanted me to stay at the prison. He wanted me to try to stick it out, even though the pressure was building. At the time, leaving the prison seemed like the right thing to do. Looking back, I think maybe I should've stayed. Those first three years that I was gone I had more time to spend with my dad. I spent more time with Mary, and that was priceless.

Since they have passed away and I no longer have the immense pressure of Mary's illness, I truly miss what I used to do. I wish I could go back, but there is no turning the clock back; there's no more putting the genie back in the bottle; and water doesn't flow upstream. I substitute taught for three years when I first left, looking for a job and taking classes to add to my teaching certificate.

I was also a Graduate Assistant in Sociology for a semester. My friend Maria who I had met through Tae Kwon Do was a professor at one of the local colleges, and she asked me to become her Graduate Assistant while I was taking a couple of Sociology classes. I got another major in English and, essentially, a minor in Special Education so that I could start teaching full time again.

Three years after I left Corrections, I found a great teaching job. It was in a small country school a little over 20 miles away from my home that had a fantastic Principal and a super Assistant Principal. In fact, the Assistant Principal was the daughter of a guy I had worked with at the prison. It was while I was working here that my dad would die the second day of the first semester and Mary would die the second to last day of the first semester. I left that job after the school year was up, I just was lost.

Since I couldn't have my old drug of choice, adrenaline, my new drug of choice became endorphins from working out. While I was going to school and subbing, I was doing my Tae Kwon Do in the evenings four and five times a week. I would do my Stairmaster between 40-60 minutes a day and I set it so that it was between 60-80 steps per minute. The crazy thing was I was doing 1,000 sit-ups and 500 pushups while I was watching TV in the evenings. I was in great shape, almost to the point of over training, but it was a good high for me. I enjoyed it.

Over those three years, Mary slowly went downhill. It was hard to watch. Ironically as I physically improved, Mary went downhill.

It was almost as if I was trying to build strength to give her which I prayed that God would let me do. I knew it didn't make sense but I was beside myself with grief and worry.

The last three-plus years that Mary was alive, we didn't have sex. The elasticity that a body needs to function correctly was gone in Mary. She had congestive heart failure, because her heart wasn't beating right. Sometimes her bowel movements would pain her, because her bowels didn't have the elasticity for peristaltic movement, and neither did her sex organs.

So it was a sexless marriage, but I understood, I truly did. If she had just not been in the mood or been cold and not wanting to do it, I'd have probably gone insane and ballistic, probably been a horrible jerk. But I knew she couldn't help it, and so that was something I just had to deal with.

We talked a lot, but I could tell she was pulling away from me again. She didn't want to be close when she died. She wanted to try to ease my pain. Our relationship had been sort of back and forth, getting closer, pulling back, getting closer, pulling back, sort of like the tides of the ocean, only ours were the tides of the cancer count.

I was able to manage my beast and my anger at this time, although when I first left Corrections, I remember the first day I was walking to class with Maria. Some student saw her from over a block away and started running towards her and hollering, and since I had just come from Corrections, I sort of went into Corrections mode, as my daughter calls it. As the student came running closer and closer, I stepped in front of Maria, sort of in a protective stance, and in my mind I was thinking when he got close enough, I was just going to give him a tiger claw to the throat, knock him down and then see what happened. My gentle side was able to convince me that this wasn't an attack, we weren't inside the walls of a maximum security prison, and to chill out a little bit.

It was also during this time that I coached Tom in wrestling and two or three days of the week, I would take Tom and Sarah to Tae Kwon Do with me. Tom would eventually get his third degree black belt, and at present, he's preparing for his fourth degree black belt so he can be a Tae Kwon Do Master.

Sarah was ready to test for her second degree black belt when my dad died. She's gone back a few times but never has been able to develop the passion that she once had.

So during these three years that I was substitute teaching and taking classes, I grew closer with Tom and Sarah, and that is priceless. We talked a lot more. We were able to understand each other more. We became a team knowing that Mommy was going to die.

It was strange that my life didn't revolve around the Pontiac Correctional Center or the Department of Corrections. I didn't get called in the middle of the night anymore and didn't get calls on the weekend that a pop machine was broken. It was unfamiliar. I enjoyed taking the classes. It helped to distract me. I found that if I was distracted, life was easier.

This was something else I now started to do - to distract myself, to occupy my mind, to make it work. Sometimes I did a puzzle, sometimes I just did research. I enjoyed doing term papers again. It kept my mind busy, and I wanted to be distracted. I wanted to be distracted throughout the day and sleep at night. I didn't want to think, I didn't want to feel.

It was also during this time I helped my dad campaign for City Council. The City of Pontiac had elected a new mayor in the primaries, and my dad was running in the general election. The City seemed to be in some turmoil. The old mayor had wanted to create a salary for the mayor of about $70,000 a year, and the town was in an uproar. The new mayor had won by a landslide.

Since my dad was running for election against a very nice lady who was very popular but had supported the previous mayor, it was an interesting campaign. In the end, my dad won by two votes, and he enjoyed it. He savored that victory which would be his last political victory.

I had two different semester-long teaching jobs that were long-term sub jobs, and I enjoyed the kids and I enjoyed teaching. I felt I was able to connect with some of the behaviorally-disordered kids quite well. Coming from Corrections, I understood their thinking. I tried to give them some examples, real life examples, of why they should change their poor behavior choices and study, but I still had trouble with myself, because I was in DOC mental mode. I was much more aggressive than the average teacher in my discussions and my arguments and my confrontations with my students. And with teachers, I was in much more of a collaborative work force and mode than that of the leadership role that I was used to.

I encountered a couple of people when I was teaching that just rubbed me the wrong way and I thought were wrong. They were good people and I make no judgments of them.

One person felt that she had to give the students the answers, because the students might otherwise fail. This teacher's aide had a

150

whole file drawer from 30 years of being a teacher's aide of copies of tests with answers. Her philosophy was, "If we can just get these kids good grades until they're old enough to understand that they have to study, then we'll have helped them."

I disagreed. I thought we needed to start teaching the students at the beginning of the year, and they got the grade that they earned. If they didn't earn a good enough grade, that should motivate them to earn a better grade.

I also experienced another educational professional who felt that we should help the students even outside of the classroom. This Principal asked me to take home some sports uniforms to wash in my personal washing machine, which I refused. Mary's blood counts were low. She was very susceptible to diseases and sicknesses, and I certainly wasn't going to bring other people's dirty and germy laundry into our home!

So I struggled a little bit to find the right job and the right fit. I finally found what I thought was the perfect teaching job that I could stay with for 15 or 20 years until I retired from teaching. It was a little country school and a great job, a great fit, and I loved everything about it. My two bosses were wonderful. I enjoyed them. The Principal was a great guy and the Assistant Principal was a great gal.

151

I enjoyed teasing her from time to time, because I had worked with her dad at the prison.

Right before school started, Mary helped me decorate my classroom at the end of the summer. I was falling into the mode of the status quo with her and with our life together. I hoped it would stay this way. Things weren't great, but I was able to survive.

Dr. Hough had told me when I got my physical that summer not to build up my hopes that things would stay the same. He reminded me that Mary was going to die and not to let it shock me or stun me since it had taken longer than the doctors had thought. He wanted me to be prepared, and in my mind I thought I was prepared. I had left my stressful job. I was doing something that I enjoyed, teaching kids. But in the end, I wasn't prepared for that fall at all.

Dad when he was in the US Navy, 1948 to 1952.

Dad. Mom, and me 1962.

CHAPTER TWELVE

<u>My Dad.</u>

My dad was born on March 30, 1930, five months after the crash of '29 and the start of the Great Depression. He was born on a farm in rural Flannigan, the third of three boys. He lived with his two brothers, his mom and dad, and his grandpa and grandma, and during the Depression all seven of them lived off the 80-acre farm.

His two older brothers went in the Navy and Dad copied them when he got out of high school. He was a star athlete and actually got a basketball scholarship to Eureka College in 1948, but he decided to go in the Navy instead. He became a flight engineer on the big four engine bombers that the Navy had. They were the Navy version of the B-24 Liberator Bomber that the Army used.

My dad was my hero. To me he was the toughest guy alive. All little kids I guess, all little boys especially, think their dad is the toughest person around. But some of the things my dad did still amaze me. He actually passed the test when he was in the Navy to be a frogman, a Navy Seal. When he found out that he had to sign up for two more years in the Navy, he decided not to do it.

He met my mom in 1954 and they got married in 1956. I was born four years later in 1960. He worked heavy equipment and construction all his life. He became my best friend somewhere between college and getting married. In some ways, I think he was a self-made man. He built his own business, sold it in 1984 and then went to work for the State of Illinois Highway Department for the last 13 years he worked, retiring at 67.

Throughout my life, my dad taught me honesty, honor, the love of God, and the love of country. He taught me how the world worked and how people worked. He taught me how to be strong. When I was in high school as a freshman, I didn't want to go out for wrestling. I went out for freshman football, and I just wasn't mature enough for my age, I guess, to compete or to stay competitive. But he wouldn't hear of me not going out for wrestling. In a lot of ways, he shamed me into going out for wrestling. I still remember he told me that I had to get tough so I could protect my family someday, and I told him, "Well, I know how to protect my family," and as freshman in high school would do, I argued back. But he ended up winning, and I always thought about that argument throughout the rest of my life. My dad challenged me to be tough and to be able to protect my family, and to this day, I think about that when I work out. It still drives me at 50 to stay in shape and be physically fit. Days that I don't want to work out, days that I don't want to take care of myself, I think of that, and it usually is enough to motivate me.

My dad got involved in politics long before I was born. He liked working for the Republican Party, and throughout his life as he lived in our small town of Pontiac, he did a lot of community service. For years, he was on the Fourth of July Committee. He helped all of the Veterans Groups with their honor guards for funerals and different functions for raising the flags. He was a Precinct Committeeman for the Republican Party for a long, long time, and he served a couple of terms on the City Council.

He taught me to give to other people that weren't as fortunate, and as he lived his life, he taught me more lessons than I can remember. As time went on and Mary got sick and dad retired, the last remaining years of his life he spent helping Mary, me, Tom and Sarah.

Up until the end, his health was good. He was strong and sharp. In fact, the beginning of that summer when his health deteriorated, he was walking two miles. During Mary's illness, he helped me paint the house, every room and all the outside, and then over the years as Mary continued her battle with cancer and she wanted different projects done, he would do them. It takes a lot of work to keep an old house fixed up and looking nice, but Dad enjoyed it, and it was great for me because then I didn't have to worry about it. I could really depend on my dad.

But then that last summer, his health started going down. The beginning of April we were sitting at our kitchen table talking, having a meal, Mary, Tom, Sarah, my mom, dad, and me.

My dad said, "You know, I must be getting old. I get halfway through my two-mile walk, and I have to stop for a little bit and catch my breath. It just gets a little tight in the middle of my chest," as he rubbed it.

In May, as his health seemed to go down a little bit, my dad went and got a stress test. He thought if there was something wrong, he'd catch it early. They didn't find anything. He was fine for a 77-year-old man. Throughout June he shortened his walks, and stopped by the doctor's office three and four times a week to have his blood pressure checked, because that's what Dr. Hough thought it was. They switched his medicine a couple of times, but still he had tightness in his chest, and it was starting to hurt. In July, he actually stopped his walks. He rode the bike quite a bit with my daughter, Sarah, but he still had chest pains from time to time if he exerted himself.

When August rolled around, he insistently asked Dr. Hough for more tests. They did more extensive diagnostic work, including some dye tests with the stress tests. Again, it came back that he was fine for a 77-year-old man. There were a few abnormalities, but nothing to worry about.

When we celebrated my mom's birthday a couple days early on Sunday, August 12, 2007, my dad and I were sitting on the back patio talking. We were talking about politics like we normally did, and I was telling dad about testing for the first part of my Fourth Degree Black Belt. By that fall, I would be a Tae Kwon Do Master. I thought having my Fourth Degree Black Belt would be cool. Dad was proud of me. I recalled the conversation he had with me when I was a freshman in high school about having to be tough enough and strong enough and smart enough and able enough to protect my family and myself. I guess now that I was going to be a Tae Kwon Do Master he seemed satisfied and confident that I could do that, protect myself and his grandkids.

I still remember that conversation. We were focused on Mary, trying to figure out when she was going to die because her health was going down, planning what to do after she was gone and how Dad was going to help me. We ended up talking about his last tests, and he still wasn't satisfied. He told me that if he dropped dead of a heart attack, he wanted me to sue whoever was reading the tests, because he didn't believe that he was fine. He thought he might have to have some kind of stent or bypass, to be "cleaned out" as he put it.

I told him that Mary had a lot of tests and they were really accurate, and that I believed what the tests said, what the doctors said. I should've done more at the time. I look back and I'm racked with guilt. I wish I'd have taken him to a hospital. I wish I'd have gone with him to the tests.

I thought God couldn't do any more to me, and at the time, I just didn't think that God would take my dad from me. I couldn't handle any more. I'd given up my career in Corrections. Mary was going to die, we knew that. We knew she was getting worse. It was a matter of months. I just couldn't believe that God would take Dad from me. But a few nights later we had our last talk. It was Monday August 20, 2007, and the Thursday before, Mary had had chemo. Mary hadn't felt good all day on that Monday. She was nauseous and couldn't eat, and she called up my dad to see if he would make her some mashed potatoes.

By the time I got home from work, he was there. It had been my first day of teaching with the students. Dad had just brought in the potatoes and was walking out the door, but all of a sudden, he had to sit down on our steps. He had the look of pain on his face. I asked him what was wrong, and he said his chest hurt, and I was stunned. The pit in my stomach just froze. My intestines were in a knot. I couldn't really grasp what he was saying.

Part of me said, "Oh, my God! He's going to have a heart attack!"

Part of me thought, "This can't be happening."

I told him that we needed to call 911, and he said no, because he had a City Council meeting. It would be fine, it would go away. He didn't want to make a big deal out of it. He was going to see a cardiologist on Wednesday, two days later, and he didn't think it was a big deal.

When he got done with the City Council meeting about 8:15, he stopped by our house. He knew Mary wasn't feeling well, so he called me on my cell phone and said, "Hey, come on out and sit in the pickup truck and talk to me."

We did that a lot so that we wouldn't bother Mary when she was sleeping.

We gossiped a little bit and talked about different things. My dad told me he wasn't going to run for City Council again, and that I should run. He told me that he thought the cardiologist would find something wrong with him and he'd probably have to get a stent or something cleaned out in his arteries, but that he'd do whatever he had to, so he could stay around and help me after Mary was gone. We had to get Tom and Sarah raised and he was going to help me.

The thing I remember was he reached out with his right hand and he patted my left leg, which he'd done on and off throughout the years growing up. My grandfather was a patter, too.

My dad patted my leg and he told me, "If it's my time, it's my time, Honey. Don't feel too bad."

I pleadingly responded to him that he had to stick around and help me and that I wasn't going to be able to do it by myself. The last words I said to him as I got out of the pickup truck were, "I love you, Dad. I'll see you tomorrow," and he said, "Love you, too, Honey." Then I never talked to him again.

The next day Dad worked in his yard and in the garden a little bit. In the afternoon he came over to mow my yard with his riding lawn mower. My son, Tom, was there to help. He said Papa was happy and talking to some of the neighbors who stopped to visit as he was mowing. It seemed like my dad knew everybody. He represented this neighborhood for over 30 years as a Precinct Committeeman and six years as a City Councilman.

When he got done mowing the yard, he was going home to work in his garden some more. About a half hour later that's where my mom found him sitting on the swing in their backyard next to the garden. He didn't look quite right, she said. He looked sort of gray and ashen. He told her he didn't feel real well and asked her if she could take the cucumbers in the basement.

They walked in the house and he sat in his chair. He asked my mom for an aspirin and by the time she got it and brought it back, he asked her to take him to the hospital. He thought he was having a heart attack. He went to sit on the porch while she pulled the car out of the garage. When she got out of the garage, he told her that she needed to call the ambulance. As mom ran in the house to call the ambulance, I was driving down the street. I wanted to check on Dad to see how he was doing. I was concerned. I knew he had his cardiologist appointment the next day.

About two and a half blocks down the street, I saw my dad's face look at me and then he started to stand up as I was driving down the street. It looked like he did some deep knee bends, two or three, and then as I was pulling in the driveway in what was extreme slow

162

motion, I saw my dad who was 6'3" tall buckle at the knees and start to fall, and as he fell, his knees hit the porch floor and then his torso fell even further and hit the concrete stairs. I can still remember as I write this how my dad's head and right arm bounced, just like a deflated ball, on the concrete stairs as he fell down.

I was dismayed, and horrified. Panic like I'd never known in my life gripped me. I accelerated into the driveway, slammed on the brakes, jumped out of my Trailblazer, left the door open and I was screaming, "Dad! Dad!"

There was terror in my voice, I could hear it. I wanted to cry. I wanted to call for help. I wanted to run away. I didn't want to face this. But I knew I had to act, that there was no one else. Fear that I'd never known in my entire life gripped me. I had to pick my dad up and lay him down on the porch and started CPR.

Now I'm a big guy at 6'4" but my dad was a big guy at 6'3". When they talk about dead weight, they mean dead weight. It took me a couple of tries to get him with a good grip. I picked him up and laid him down on the porch. I still remember that his left eye rolled straight back and his right eye rolled straight to the right. I started doing CPR on dad. I was focused. Nothing else in the world mattered.

I knew CPR very well. I'd been a lifeguard in high school and college. Every year that I worked at the Correctional Center I had training, and every year as a school teacher I had training. In fact, four days before this, I'd had my refresher course. We even worked with an AED, automated external defibrillator.

I counted my pumps on his chest and then I did the two breaths. I counted my pumps and I did the two breaths. I kept repeating this cycle.

A couple of neighbors had seen Dad fall and they ran over. I ignored them. They tried to talk to me and I just kept counting out loud. I was thinking a million different thoughts as I did that. I was begging God not to take him, but to take me instead. I knew my dad wouldn't want this, but I thought, "I don't care." And I kept begging God not to take him at all, because I couldn't go on without my dad, without my best friend.

As I gave him mouth to mouth, I felt his whiskers. He needed a shave. He smelled like my dad always did. Some very strange and familiar memories came back to me as I was gripped in panic, wanting to cry, wanting to fly away, wanting to be anywhere else. But knowing I had to be there. Some strange old memories came back into my mind. I remembered when my dad used to whisker my belly. I remembered when he used to carry me on his shoulders. It was strange, a million different thoughts in a million different directions.

I worked on him for five to six minutes before the EMTs got there. My mom had come to the door and she was screaming at me to fix him. And I hear her voice to this day. The guilt still hits me even now when I least expect it for not saving him. He did come back for a few moments. He mumbled he was sorry and that he loved me. And then he was out.

When the EMTs arrived, they put the AED on him to see if his heartbeat was going, and the AED said "No shock needed" in its mechanical voice, he was good I prayed. I had some hope. I was still frozen with dumbfounded shock. It was like watching a TV show that was actually a nightmare.

As the ambulance took my dad to the hospital, my mom rode with me and we drove out to the hospital together. I kept praying the whole way, driving like an idiot, trying to keep up with the ambulance, but I lost it at one of the red lights. So by the time we got to the hospital, Dad was in the ER when we walked in. Mom wouldn't go in the room and I didn't want to either, but I knew I had to. There was no one else for my dad. Mary, Tom, and Sarah were on their way, but they hadn't arrived yet.

The doctors were working on him. I knew enough from Mary's time in the hospital exactly what to look at on the life monitoring machine. There was no heartbeat. I talked to the doctors about the time he went down. I looked at my watch when I started CPR as I was trained. It was 12 minutes to four when dad went down. I told them that they should probably stop working on him, because it'd been too long and my dad wouldn't want to come back in a vegetative state.

The doctor said that they had given him medicine to hopefully restart the heart, and the protocol said they had to go 30 minutes which was about five more minutes before they stopped.

I stood there next to the doctor, frequently checking my watch while keeping an eye on the machine that indicated a heartbeat. When the half hour was up, I again told the doctor to stop. It killed me to do that, but I knew that's what my dad wanted. He wouldn't want to come back and be anybody less than what he was.

When the medical team stopped working on him, the world felt like a different place. The hospital called the Coroner, and they were doing some paperwork about dad. I walked out the door and out in the parking lot and I looked around. The world was a different place. The world had simply and suddenly turned upside down. It

166

wasn't the same place it had been an hour before. It didn't have the same feel. Somehow I'd been transported into a parallel universe where everything felt wrong.

After my dad died, I was cold to my core, like when a person has a fever and can't get warm. I couldn't feel anything. I felt like I was drunk. I couldn't process thoughts. It was the most hideous feeling that I'd had in my life up to that point. I wandered around the parking lot a little bit, called a good friend who was like a brother to me, Doug, and within a few minutes he was out there to help. At that time Doug was the only one I could think of calling, he had lost his dad back in high school. Somehow I know he could help me.

The Coroner arrived and we had to talk Mom into doing an autopsy. Mary was very concerned about my health, because I had to raise Tom and Sarah. She told my mom that if the autopsy could find something out about the cause of Dad's death, that would help me, and that convinced her to allow an autopsy.

Mom didn't want to go in the hospital room when the Coroner was in there. The Coroner and I got stuff out of my dad's pockets. He was a friend to both my dad and me. We knew Mike for years, talked to him a lot at different political functions, and Mike couldn't have been nicer and kinder at this time.

We found some change, some rubber bands, an old comb, and some fingernail clippers. We got his wallet, took his watch off, and took my dad's license out of his wallet. That had to go with him to the autopsy. As we were doing this, I noticed that even though my dad had a long-sleeved, button-down, farmer-type shirt on, he still had on an old tee shirt. It was yellow and had some holes. I couldn't help but joke to Mike that I guessed that old saying was true, "Always make sure you put your best underwear on, because you never know when you're going to the hospital that last time."

We both chuckled, and Mike told me that that tee shirt had a lot of use left into it, and Dad having grown up on the farm wasn't going to throw anything away that was good.

That night at the house after Dad died a lot of friends and family came over. Mary was heartbroken, too, but she was more worried about me.

I still remember that night. I wandered around aimlessly throughout the house, in and out of the house and around the neighborhood. I couldn't accept the fact that my dad was gone.

Somehow I didn't want his pickup truck sitting at his house alone. Mom was staying at our house with us, and Dad had given me a key to the truck years before, so I drove the truck over to my house.

I felt abandoned. Mom wasn't really any help to me. Nobody was any help to me. I was alone. I was truly, truly alone. I couldn't feel. I couldn't think.

The next morning we went to make arrangements for Dad. Mary had a doctor's appointment to check her blood counts, and then Tom, Sarah and I were going to meet Mary so that we could buy Tom and Sarah some nice clothes for the funeral. Kids never seem to have the right dress clothes when they need them.

In route to meet Mary, she called to let me know that she had to be admitted to the hospital immediately. She didn't want to. She argued with the doctor, but thank goodness her mom was with her and told her she needed to go. Her blood counts were dangerously low, and the funeral preparations weren't worth her dying for.

It was hard on her to miss the services, and it was hard on me, too. I needed someone to help and to support me, and I didn't feel I could do this without Mary. Tom and Sarah were with me, but I had to pretend to be strong for them, although they saw right through it that I was crushed, and they both were very protective of me.

That first night that Mary was in the hospital, I still remember sitting on our bed at home and talking to her on the phone. I told her I didn't want to go on. I told her I didn't have strength to do anything. I told her that if a semi-truck was barreling down on me, I wouldn't have the energy or the inclination to even move. I could hear panic in her voice as she talked to me and told me I had to be there for Tom and Sarah. She told me that my dad wouldn't want this, and while I knew she was right, I didn't care. Mary tried that night to talk me into not giving up. I kept telling her that God was playing some cruel joke on me, because this just wasn't right. Dad was gone and she was dying, and I was an only child.

Somehow I made it through the next couple days. My uncle from Texas, my dad's older brother, Uncle Cal, came up with all my cousins.

My cousins, Bill and Jim, and their wives, my cousin, Faye, all came to Dad's funeral. It was an impressive funeral, in my opinion. Dad had a lot of honors bestowed on him from the Veterans' group. They had a fallen soldier ceremony that they normally don't do at Veterans' services. They just do it for the Veterans that gave a lot. I felt honored for dad, as I stayed at the visitation and greeted people and talked to them. I thanked them for coming and realized that I didn't care if they were dressed up or not, that they showed up, that they cared.

It felt like the enormous burden of the world was on my shoulders. Everything depended on me now. I didn't want to be strong anymore. I wanted to give up, but I knew I had to get through the services for my dad. That's what he would've wanted. Mary was in the hospital, and some of her friends came to help and do things, and for that, I will forever be grateful. Mary felt horrible because she was hospitalized, and she was concerned and worried about me. She wanted to be there. She even asked the doctor if she could leave just to come to the funeral, and he said no.

The grief and despair I felt were beyond description. Physical and mental pain that I had never endured before seemed to rack my body. I had near panic attacks, and for a long time I had trouble sleeping. I paced all the time. Even after the service things didn't change. Sometimes throughout the day my stomach would hurt like somebody had smacked it with the end of a baseball bat. Physical pain like I'd never felt. I'd played football in high school. I wrestled in high school and college. I even boxed a little in college. I'd done Tae Kwon Do for over 20 years by now. I'd never been hit so hard in my life.

A couple months after dad had died, I was out at his gravesite, and it just hit me, the pain could all go away. This would be over. I pulled out my buck knife that I carried, with a 4½" long blade, and I thought, "You know, it could be over real fast."

I opened it up, pulled my shirt up and put the point against my belly button. I gripped the handle, and I thought, "You know what? If I'm going to do it, I'm going to do it like a man. I take Tae Kwon Do. I'll at least kill myself like martial artists do. I shove this knife in as far as it will go and with the last of my strength, I'll yank it to the right."

I was right-handed. I had the sharp side aimed to the right, and I gripped it. And I kept thinking, "Just push. Just push fast and hard. One swift stroke and it will be done."

But somehow I heard my dad's voice in the back of my mind telling me that the kids needed me, especially Sarah who was still so young. And then the little Christian voice in my head told me suicide was a sin. If I wanted to see Dad, I couldn't do this. My faith was almost broken. I wasn't mad at God, but I couldn't believe He had done this to me. I felt abandoned by God. My faith was hanging by a thread. It looked like a frayed rope in my mind.

That afternoon I didn't kill myself. I still remember thinking that I was mad at Mary. I was tired of her being sick. She needed to stay alive and carry the burden. I was tired of being the one who seemed to bear all of the responsibility. I was tired of being the strong one. I wanted to be weak. I didn't want to go on. I was pissed off that I had to do this.

But inside of me, my beast was roaring, trying to fire me up and get me to go on and find some strength. My Christian side tried to keep telling me to have faith, that everything happens for a reason, and this was God's plan. But I didn't care. My faith was hanging by a thread. Then I thought of the suffering that Christ had gone through for me as my personal savior. I folded up the knife and disgustedly put it back in my pocket.

Over the next few months I struggled every day, every hour, and every minute, to move forward. I went through some of my grandparents' old pictures and scanned them into the computer. I thought that this little project might help me. I could give the pictures to my cousins and post them on computer for all the family to see. It was a good chance to remember the life lessons that my Grandpa and Grandma Stalter had taught me, and what my dad had taught me and had told me to hold on to for hope in the future.

A little voice inside my head kept telling me there was something worthwhile ahead of me to live for hope in the future. Somewhere past the horizon there was a normal life again. Someday Mary would be gone, and while it would be hard, I would find that life that I wanted. I would find that life that I had early on with Mary. A normal life that most people take for granted, but that I realized was the most precious thing on the planet. A wife who loved me, one who was healthy and whole.

Uncle Cal, (Dad's brother), Mom, Tom, Me, and Sarah at Dad's funeral.

CHAPTER THIRTEEN

<u>Mary's Death.</u>

Mary came home from the hospital a week after Dad died. It was Tuesday, August 28, 2007. As we were driving home from the hospital, she told me that this was probably why she was still here, why she had lived longer than the doctors' expectations. She was here to help me get over losing dad. Her concern for me was evident and it was overwhelming. Part of me wondered if it was for me or if it was for our kids, because her concern was that I had to be strong for the kids. I had to stay here for the kids. I had to take care of the kids. Or was it for both of those reasons? I wasn't sure.

She grew closer to me. She didn't have any more chemo until the end of October. I think somehow she knew that I was contemplating taking my own life, but I never told her. She didn't try to push away anymore, to ease her coming death. Mary had been emotionally distancing herself from me so that when she did die I wouldn't feel so bad. She had told me this months before one time when I was asking why she was being so cold one day. She was scared for me, and I knew it.

My mom was staying at our house. She'd sleep at our house at night. During the day, she went to her house and tended her garden, did her work in the house, but she just didn't want to stay there alone. Mary was very good about that. When Mary started back on chemo at the end of October, Mom went back to sleeping at her house, because Mary would move from one location to another. She would sleep in the bed for an hour, go to a chair, go the couch, and go to a different chair. She just couldn't sleep in one spot. The chemo bothered her.

Mary began requiring more time in the hospital every other week starting in November until she died. She would be in a week and then home a week, one time she was in the hospital for two weeks. She had problems eating. Her internal organs were swelling because the cancer was in the liver. The doctors discovered it right before Thanksgiving. Mary's liver was very swollen, pushing all the other organs around inside her, and that was why she was having trouble eating, why she was in a lot of pain.

The first part of December I had asked Mary how she was doing, how much time she thought she had. I'd asked her this for several years. She had said, "A lot," or "I don't know." Now she said, "I don't know if I can make it to the end of the month if I keep going downhill the way I am."

That shocked me. I realized I had to pick myself up and carry the burden again, to be strong for everyone. I had to be strong again for the whole family. Mary had tried for those three months after Dad had died, but now she was just failing too fast and was becoming too weak.

Tom tried to lighten the burden and help. He tried to be strong for me and he was strong. I had seen the fear in his eyes when I was talking to Mary on the phone after Dad had died and she was in the hospital. He had never seen me weak before. It bothers me to this day. I used to joke with the kids when they were younger that I was a terminator just like Arnold Schwarzenegger was in the movies, that nothing could hurt me, that I'd last forever, and I'd always be strong. I guess Tom realized I really wasn't a terminator after all.

Our last Christmas was tough. We had a Christmas Eve dinner planned and Mary had come home on the 23rd. I knew it was going to be Mary's last Christmas Eve. I wanted a distraction so I wanted her family there, too.

Mary's parents had been with us different Christmas Eves on and off over the years, and they all brought the food. Mary didn't have to do anything. But Mary was the type of woman that wanted to cook.

She wanted to help. She wanted to make her guests feel at home, and she couldn't. She couldn't do anything and that upset her.

It was a hard dinner for me. I was sad that my dad was gone and I knew Mary was close to death. We could all sense it. The place felt like there was an angel of death walking around. We all knew that she couldn't last much longer.

Mary had given each of us a Christmas card. It was her last Christmas card. She gave one to me and she gave one to every member of her family. Each one was different.

Mary's Christmas cards were self-made. She'd done them on our computer. She liked playing with the computer.

The last week that she was alive and home, she also organized all her files. She made things neat and easy for me to find, explained to me where everything was for Sarah's 4-H and for Tom's different projects at school. She made it simple for me to find when she was gone. She even took the time to show me how to work her camera.

She'd made her cards on Print Shop. She had a nativity scene on the front of them that said, "Joy to the World." The back of the card said, "Created Especially for you With Christmas Love by Mary Stalter."

When I got my card, I wasn't sure what it would say, the typical "I love you. You are a great husband" or something to that effect. All the normal stuff you read when you go to the Hallmark Shop. I noticed that Mary's sisters and her mom and dad were choked up, so as I opened my card, the last one to do so, I started reading.

It said, "As I reflect, I find that I am especially blessed and thankful to be celebrating God's gift to us, His Son, Jesus Christ who was sent to us so that we may have eternal life. I'm exceptionally grateful to be surrounded by such a wonderful family.

Mike, you are the perfect partner for me. There is no one better for me to have shared my life with. You make me laugh and have been my rock to lean on through all of the good and all of the bad. Your strength and constant love have always been there throughout our marriage every step of the way, and when it feels like I am sinking in quicksand, you have always been there to pull me back so I can keep going.

No words can adequately express how precious you are to me and how much I love you. Thank you for all of the things you have done and continue to do for me. Love always and forever, Mary."

The week before Christmas when Mary was in the hospital, she had had her chemo port taken out. It had become infected. They'd only put it in a few months before, but her systems were failing and the port had become infected. In fact, the site of the old port had become infected, so they had to open that up.

So Mary had what looked like two gaping wounds made by the claws of a tiger in her chest. They were about three inches long, one to one and one-half inches deep. There was black, dead skin and red, infected skin draining pus, green and white.

I had to clean these incisions out three times a day, starting on December 23rd when Mary came home. The second time I was cleaning them, Mary started crying. She said she was afraid she would have to go into a nursing home because she didn't think that I could do this. She mentioned me passing out when Tom was born, and I told her, "That's true, but I know I have to do this," and I wasn't going to let her go into a nursing home.

I'd have to take the old yucky gauze out, get a little squirt bottle with some saline solution and medicine in it, squirt it around in the holes, in the slices, the cuts, and then repack it with gauze and tape the bandaging up. Mary was very grateful that I could do this.

She could hardly go up the stairs the last few months that she was alive, and I remember her last trip up the stairs. It took her about 20 minutes to go up 18 stairs. She would walk up one or two and stand for a minute or two, take another step or two and stop, lean on the rail all the way up. I don't know how long she was upstairs, but it wasn't very long, 15-20 minutes. I had to go upstairs for something and she was starting to come down. She decided to sit down and slide down the stairs on her rear, but that still wore her out.

I got whatever I needed upstairs, and started down the stairs, too. She had gone down two or three steps and was sitting there, so I just sat behind her and we talked. Every three or four minutes she'd slide down another stair, and so it took us a while to get down.

Every time I walked by those stairs for the rest of the time I lived in that house, I remembered the last time Mary went up and down them.

Mary had her last chemo treatment the Thursday after Christmas. That night when she came home, she was feeling fairly good. She didn't have quite the rush from the steroids that they gave her with the chemo treatment that she normally did, but she was fairly perky and talkative. We sat around in the living room with the TV off and talked for about two and a half hours. Then she went to sleep with a busy day ahead the next day.

Her friends from high school who had visited her every couple of months for the last several years made a girls' day of it, and were coming to see her the next morning, Friday. That same afternoon she was going to go to the oncologist and get a shot to help build up her blood counts.

During the time that she was visiting with her friends, our lawyer came to the house. Mary had wanted to make sure that she had her Will signed before she died. She wanted to make sure that things were done the way she wanted regarding a number of different things.

The next morning, Saturday, I went to Tae Kwon Do and was awarded my Fourth Degree Black Belt. I had taken the test in November and my belt had arrived, so it was presented to me. I was now officially a Tae Kwon Do Master. I brought it home that afternoon all excited. I showed it to Mary. She was starting to get tired. Her blood counts were dropping from the chemo. She looked exhausted. But she smiled and said that was really good, that she was proud of me, and that was about all she said. It wasn't until after she died that I found out she talked about it more than I was aware of with other people and thought about it more.

A kid named Ethan who took Tae Kwon Do lessons with me from Master Kim had a mother who worked as an X-ray technician. She had done two or three of the last X-rays on Mary, and they knew each other from the son and me doing Tae Kwon Do together. Mary had told Ethan's mom how proud she was of me and what an accomplishment it was and she seemed to go on and on, according to Ethan's mom.

But at the time, to me Mary seemed rather indifferent about my accomplishment. "That's really nice. I'm proud of you."

I was disappointed that Mary hadn't told that to me, but I was grateful that Ethan's mom told me even if it was after Mary died. Mary never gave me a lot of praise during our marriage and I don't know why. Most of the time it never bothered me but here at the end of her life it did. That's why her last Christmas card meant so much to me. She was letting me go and not wanting me to hold on to the past.

We woke up Sunday morning, Mary's last day at our house. She was weak, very weak. Her mom and dad came to visit that afternoon. Mary was sitting in the kitchen. I had just changed her bandages and she was tired. She started to cry in front of her mom and dad. She was just that exhausted and that tired from fighting for 17½ years. I suggested to Mary that we should called Dr. Jeong and see what he wanted to do, but she didn't want to go to the hospital. She tried to hang out and be tough. I think in her mind she knew it would be her last trip. But she finally gave in about 10:30 at night.

I drove Mary to the hospital. We picked up her sister to go with us so that she could walk with Mary into the hospital while I parked the vehicle. That was a long last week. The first couple of days in the hospital, Mary didn't want to see any people at all. She didn't want to talk to anybody. She didn't want any calls, and she made it clear to me to tell everybody not to call. When someone had called, Mary reached me at home and chewed me out.

Mary seemed to be a little bit better on Wednesday. I saw her every day that week except Thursday. Thursday I had to meet with a lawyer regarding my dad's cause of death. I was convinced that the doctors had read the results from his heart tests incorrectly. I remembered the last thing Dad had told me on that day we were celebrating Mom's birthday. "If I just drop dead, sue the shit out of them." So I didn't see Mary that Thursday, I was talking to the lawyer.

Eventually, I found out that there was nothing we could have done for Dad and the doctors did everything right, which made me feel

184

better. But the long and short of it was that Dad had some blockage from years of high blood pressure, and too much cholesterol with some blockage from that. There wasn't enough blockage that the doctors would have done a bypass surgery, but there was enough blockage that it disrupted his electrical circuits, sort of like his heart just short-circuited. My Grandpa Stalter had died that way, but he was almost 87, Dad had only been 77.

Friday, January 4, 2008, was our 23rd wedding anniversary, and I didn't know what to do for it. I went to visit her that morning. I joked with her about taking the tubes out and celebrating our anniversary with the door locked so the nurses couldn't come in. She laughed a little bit at that and told me that she knew that I wouldn't be able to have sex, because I was probably too stressed. We both laughed, realizing that was the truth. Plus we joked about all the tubes going in and out of Mary that would get in the way.

Not knowing what else to do, I had taken our wedding album to the hospital. I thought if nothing else, we could sit there and look at that and reminisce. Mary turned a couple of the pages, but after that, she was too weak to do so, so I had to. It was both sad and rewarding to sit there with her at the end of her life and look at our wedding pictures, remembering our life together.

The next day, Saturday, January 5, 2008 was Sarah's birthday. Tom and I ended up going to Sarah's basketball game. She was a cheerleader and she wanted to do some extra special flips that Mary had wanted to see her do when she'd been practicing. So I took the video camera and Sarah was a little trooper. She did some flips that she hadn't done before, and once she got them down, she just kept doing them and doing them. Every time there was a break in the game, her coach would send her out on the floor to do the flips so I could video them for Mary.

When the game was over, Tom, Sarah and I drove to the hospital for Sarah's birthday party, her 13th. We had a cake. A couple of Mary's sisters were there, along with Mary's parents, and Mary's two nieces. It was a somber birthday. Mary didn't eat any cake. The rest of us all had the cake and ice cream in the waiting room on the hospital floor, but Sarah took her presents in to open in front of Mary, and then after that, I plugged in the video camera to the TV so Mary could see Sarah doing her flips.

Mary perked up for a little bit. She had coached Sarah on how to do her flips, how to move, what to tuck here and there and other things that I did not understand from gymnastics. Mary had a background in gymnastics; she had taken lessons for several years when she was young. Plus she had worked with Sarah in gymnastics from the time Sarah was three. It was pleasant to watch the video and see Mary smile one last time. I had considered doing the video later in the week at another game, but I sensed, "You just never know," so I will always be glad that I did it on that game.

Mary was starting to feel weaker. When we first arrived there at the hospital, they were just cleaning her up. She had lost control of her bowels and had messed the bed. She was very embarrassed, and she realized that the end was near.

We made plans for having a family member stay with Mary. It was going to be her sister the first few days and then they'd rotate. I was going to stay home with the kids, because we really didn't want the kids home alone in case we got a call that we had to go to the hospital to be there when Mary passed.

Mary's sisters and her parents left. Her sister was going to go home, pack her bags and come back. Mary's two nieces, stayed there in the hospital cleaning up from the party while I was in the hospital room with Mary. I had been pressing the morphine drip for Mary. She was too weak to do it herself. One of the nurses had said something to me that it was illegal for me to press the morphine button, and I could be arrested for that. I think I gave her the coldest,

187

hardest look I'd ever given any inmate and told her I didn't care, that they could come arrest me if they wanted to try. The nurse didn't press the issue.

Right after that Mary looked up at me. She grabbed my arm with a very weak grip and said that I needed to help her. She was in too much pain, and the drugs weren't working. At first, I thought she wanted me to kill her, and I was petrified. I told her that I didn't know what to do, and she said, "Call the doctor. Call Dr. Jeong."

I said "Okay I would."

The nurse that Mary had at the time knew Mary from the Cancer Center. She was one of Mary's nurses that gave her chemo at Dr. Jeong's office and she picked up some overtime on the weekends at the hospital. I called Dr. Jeong and asked if there was something that we could do, something that we could give Mary to go to sleep with so she wouldn't be in so much pain. Dr. Jeong said there was, and he called the nurse. The nurse started crying. The drugs would make Mary comatose until the end. She wouldn't be able to talk to us. It was like putting the family dog to sleep. But Mary had heard the nurse say that she'd be comatose till the end, and Mary kept repeating she wanted to be comatose.

It took 15 or 20 minutes to get the drugs. Her nieces had come in the room by then. Tom and Sarah were there with me. The nurse administered the drugs in an IV, and Mary talked to all of us a little bit, and then she fell asleep. Her nieces stayed for about 20 minutes and then they said they were going to go home. When they went to leave, they patted Mary on the shoulders thinking that she was out for the rest of her life, but she woke up. Her eyes popped open, a little startled, jerked her head and scared the shit out of all of us.

Mary said goodbye to her nieces then and talked to Tom, Sarah and me for a few minutes. Her last words to all three of us as a group were that she loved us and she'd see us again in heaven.

Then she said something more to me, specifically to me, as I moved a little bit to one of the sides of the bed. She uttered, "You were the most important thing in my life, never let anyone convince you otherwise. I love you." And then she closed her eyes and slept. Mary never spoke again; she never opened her eyes again.

By then it was 8:30 P.M., January 5, 2008.

A little after 10 P.M. as Tom and Sarah and I were getting ready to leave I was talking with someone about Mary. Tom was listening to the conversation. Sarah, however, was looking at Mary,

189

and she was looking at her with an odd expression on her face. And all of a sudden Sarah said, "Mom's blowing bubbles. They look like red bubbles."

Sarah had seen the blood bubbles in Mary's mouth, so we got the nurse, and the nurse said it wasn't very good, that we shouldn't leave. So we stayed to be with Mary to the end.

Tom and Sarah, one of Mary's sisters and I were there. Mary's sister called the rest of Mary's family. Mary's cousin, had been talking to me throughout the day to see how Mary was doing, and I told her what was going on. They lived in a suburb of Chicago. She had been very close to Mary when she was young and still was, so she and her husband drove down from Chicago and got there about midnight.

Mary was in incredible pain even though she was sleeping and comatose. She was moaning and wailing, even though she was in this drug-induced sleep. When I talked to my mom on the phone to tell her how Mary was doing, she could hear Mary moaning and wailing, and my mom started to cry, knowing that Mary was in so much pain. It seemed that her breathing got worse and worse until it leveled off about 2 A.M., January 6th. Then, for about a half hour, it stayed about the same.

The nurse would come in to check Mary every so often, every five or 10 minutes. About 2:45, for some reason, the nurse realized that Mary still had oxygen going to her through a nasal tube. The nurse said that the oxygen was all that was keeping her alive. The nurse looked at me and said, "Do you want me to turn off the oxygen?"

Her hand started to reach for the shut-off valve but then stopped. Our eyes locked for two to three seconds before I answered, but those two or three seconds seemed like an eternity.

All of a sudden I heard hundreds of voices in my head. My brain was like a super computer. It was flooded. Adrenaline flooded through me. I had an incredible urge to protect Mary. I wanted to inject my life force, my willpower into Mary and make her better, to keep her going. As many, many thoughts raced through my head, my beast was there. He was a mirror image of me, as was my gentle self, and both my beast and my gentle self looked at me.

I heard my deceased grandparents, all of them, talking to me about the life lessons they had shared with me from the time I was little until they had passed, of hard times and hard decisions. I even remembered different TV and movie scenes I had watched throughout my life centered on hard decisions making tough choices, and those were racing through my mind.

But of all the voices I heard in my head, I heard two voices above the others. One was my dad telling me at 14 that I needed to be tough. I needed to be strong. I needed to go out for wrestling to learn how to protect my family. But the most overriding voice I heard was Mary's begging me to help her from a few hours earlier and feeling her weak grip on my arm. The decision was that I was killing her, even though I was having the nurse do it by my order.

All the years that I had wrestled in high school and college, the couple years I'd boxed in college, and the 21 years I had taken Tae Kwon Do, I'd wanted to train myself to fight, to be tough, to be strong, to make sure I could fight my way out of a cell house if it ever went down and live. And now I can kill somebody by using just words. Would the kids hate me? Would they blame me later? Would I go to hell? Those thoughts went through my mind. Was this nothing more than murder, me telling the nurse to turn the oxygen off?

I knew I could kill if I had to. Years before when Mary and I were first married, we went to her parent's farm to water the garden and feed the farm cats while they were on vacation. I hadn't really wanted to go. My hay fever was killing me at the time. I was

192

sneezing and watery-eyed and had a running nose, and I wanted to stay home in the air-conditioning. But Mary kept bugging me and wanting me to go, so I said okay. I would take my mini 14 rifle and do some target shooting while she watered the garden and fed the cats. I was going to stay away from the garden and the plants.

When we got there, I pulled in the driveway and Mary went into the house. I popped the trunk of the car and started loading my clip with bullets. I had four or five bullets in the clip when I heard Mary scream. The first thing I thought of was that she had seen a skunk or a raccoon that had gotten in the house somehow. Then I heard Mary yelling some more and I heard the garage door open. She ran out. She was terrified. The look on her face was just pure terror. Mary, being always politically correct even when she was scared, screamed at me that there was a Hispanic man in the house.

I had just completed the Illinois Department of Corrections Training Academy, and I was a little paranoid at the time. Somehow in my mind I thought that there were probably three or four people breaking into the house. Because it was a farmhouse, one person wouldn't be in there alone stealing. It was almost like a comic nightmare. I had a high-powered rifle with an almost-empty clip.

193

I put one more bullet in the clip, popped the clip in the gun, chambered a round, and aimed the gun at the house. It happened in just a fraction of a second. I knew that if somebody came out running after Mary, I'd made up my mind I was going to drop them. I was going to aim for the center of their chest and pull the trigger.

Luckily, nobody came out after Mary. We went down to the end of the lane. Mary went to get help while I stood guard to make sure nobody stole any farm equipment, and they caught the guy later. From that experience, I knew that I could kill somebody if I had to, which scared me, and now I was actually going to kill somebody. I was going to kill my wife, the mother of my children.

In the end, Mary's voice won out. I knew I had to save her from the pain no matter what, no matter what the cost was to me. In those two or three seconds, I had all of those thoughts flooding through me, and I told the nurse, "Turn it off."

I remember at the time that Tom and Sarah were looking at me, and I'm not sure where everybody else was looking.

As soon as I said "Turn it off," my beast turned into a werewolf, like the one from the movie *Underworld*, changing into a Lycan, screaming in rage, flailing his arms, wanting to smash everything that was breakable within sight. My gentle side merely sat down on the floor, legs crossed, head down and crying with a heaving chest. I, myself, however, was resolved and focused. I prayed one last time for a miracle, for God to heal her. I knew at that moment I had to stay strong.

It took 17 minutes until she died, and she died because I said for it to happen. I carry that guilt with me to this day. In some ways, I feel like I killed my wife. I killed the mother of my children. Part of me thinks I should've let the oxygen stay on until God took her, until God had her die. But I know she was in pain and when the nurse gave me the chance to end the pain, I took it.

Mary and me January 4, 1985.

CHAPTER FOURTEEN

Laying Mary to Rest.

I thought back to when I directed the nurse to turn the oxygen off, realizing that Mary was actually dead now. I started crying. My insides were raging, both my beast and my gentle side were in tears. I couldn't believe that Mary was dead. A strange thought entered my mind that all of a sudden our marriage vows were not in effect, death had parted us. I was alone!

I was also filled with anger and hate. Every sense of my being was flooded with anger and hate. I wanted to go to hell, find Satan and beat the shit out of him. If somebody would've said, "Here's the door to hell," I'd have been through it in a heartbeat. I wanted to tear him limb from limb for doing this to me, and I felt that he definitely had done it to me. I still didn't blame God, and I truly tried to understand what His plan was and why He had put me through this. But I was sad that God hadn't stepped in.

We'd all watched Mary breathe without help for those last 17 minutes. I remember Sarah crying and screaming. Tom finally broke down and cried. He had tried to stay so strong since my dad had died and to help me be strong, but now he was crying too.

I wept and wept, and I had never felt so alone in my life. I was also thinking that Dad should've been there. He was supposed to be there to help me get through this. Somehow, some way I'd been cheated out of something. As we all sat there letting the reality of Mary's death soak in, my insides grew cold. It was a numbing cold like going outside in the winter, being there too long and the subzero wind chill just knifes through the human body.

The nurses came in and asked us to leave the room. They wanted to clean up Mary. The undertaker had been called by this time and we all waited in the hallway, wandering around the hospital floor while the nurses made Mary's body look more presentable. We decided that we were going to wait for the undertaker all together, and when we went back into the room with Mary, or I should say Mary's body, because I knew her spirit was in heaven, Mary's sister wanted us all to say the Lord's Prayer.

The undertaker arrived a couple hours after he was called, and while we waited we talked about meeting later to make funeral plans. Tom, Sarah, and I left the hospital a little after 5:00 A.M. Sarah cried all the way home. It was a hard, sorrowful cry. Tom cried quietly on and off. My thoughts now changed. I hurt for Tom and

Sarah. I hurt so badly. I wanted to make it better for them, and I couldn't. I wanted to do something, anything for them, but I couldn't.

I became focused on Mary's burial and doing what she wanted for her services. It needed to be done, and I was going to do it, as well as take care of Tom and Sarah. I started calling friends, relatives and people at work that morning to let them know what happened. I also walked around the house, aimlessly. Tom and Sarah told me later that it was like I was looking for someone. Every time I walked in a room, I'd scan it and then go to another room. I think I was looking for either Dad or Mary.

Early that afternoon, Tom, Sarah and I went to the funeral home. We picked out a copper casket. It was beautiful. Mary had wanted a closed casket, so I knew we had to have a pretty one, one that looked nice. Sarah had picked out a gray one, a gray metal casket that had pink on the inside, and it was beautiful, but I reminded her that mommy wanted the casket closed. As I reflect back, I should've picked the one that Sarah wanted. It would've let Sarah feel like she had done one last thing for Mommy.

Mary's minister was going to lead the funeral services. We decided to do it at the funeral home, rather than the church. We had the casket open a half hour before visitation so family and close friends could see Mary, and then we had it closed before the public viewing. Mary was very adamant to me in our last few conversations that she didn't want people looking at her. Mary had felt very embarrassed, and humiliated in what the cancer had done to her body.

Mary had picked out some pictures for us to display. One of them was her senior picture in high school which was taken about a year and a half before I met her. Sarah seemed to be stunned that Mommy was so beautiful. She had never remembered that particular Mommy. The Mommy that she remembered had looked like a monster according to several friends and family shared descriptions, as we discussed what the cancer had done. I actually thought Mary looked more like Uncle Fester from the Addams Family. Either way, she wasn't what she was. She'd been bloated and scarred, disfigured by cancer, ravaged by a war where she was on the front lines.

When we did have the visitation, I truly was like a Rottweiler on guard duty. I was angry, I was mad, and I was going to make damn sure that I did everything Mary wanted. If somebody would've gotten in my way, I would've ripped them into minute, microscopic pieces.

There were a few people who came before the official visitation was to start. I did not know who they were, and I was so firm in sending them away that I was almost rude. I was resolved as I walked up and told them they weren't allowed to come in the room. They were very nice and understanding, staying in the back of the room. I allowed some of her high school friends who had been close to her to see Mary.

The visitation was very nice. It seemed like an unending line of people.

The morning of Mary's visitation, the town of Pontiac had had a flood. It was a flood so bad that the town was declared a federal disaster area. I was on the Pontiac City Council at the time, and many of the City workers and all City officials came through the visitation line in rubber boots and blue jeans directly from fighting the flood, and I realized that I didn't care what they looked like. As with Dad's visitation, I didn't care how people dressed, I was just touched that they remembered and wanted to pay their respects.

When I was younger and up until Dad died, I missed some visitations that I should've gone to because I didn't have time to put my dress clothes on and look proper. I don't do that now, because I know people don't care what a visitor looks like or how a funeral guest is dressed. They just appreciate the thought and the acts of kindness.

The visitation was the last time I saw Mary. When we had her casket open at the beginning of the visitation, I kissed her on her lips. Some of the family had missed seeing Mary then, so at the end of the visitation I had the funeral director open the casket for a bit more so they could see her. I stood with him at the end right before he closed it for the last time. I asked him if I had done the right thing in having the closed casket, and he nodded his head, agreed and said we had. Before he closed the casket, I looked at Mary for the last time, and I gave her one last kiss goodbye.

I had asked several people to be Mary's pallbearers, including two groomsmen from our wedding, my friends, Mark and Doug. Two co-workers who were like brothers to me, Mike and John, also served.

Mike looked upon Mary as a big sister figure. When he had been divorced and was alone at times, he would come to our house. Mary always made him feel more than welcome. Mike had once done something silly and had his tongue pierced. He subsequently found out that, as a high-level manager at the Pontiac Correctional Center, he could not appear at work with a tongue ring, and he had to take it out. That day, he came over to our house with another friend who

201

was the warden at the time, and Mary babied Mike. She got some peroxide and cleaned his tongue for him, told him what to do and how to keep it clean. Even to this day, Mike will mention that kindness to me from time to time.

Mary's three cousins were also pallbearers. And finally, and most importantly, was Mary's/our son, Tom, bearing a burden that no young man/teenager should have to carry.

Because Mary's casket was solid copper it was fairly heavy, so we had eight pallbearers.

Mary had wanted a sit-down catered dinner after the funeral service. She didn't want anybody to be inconvenienced by bringing a potluck dish to pass. The dinner was held at a local restaurant. It seemed very nice. Everyone who was at the funeral was invited. There were over a hundred people, family and friends. I had a buffet-style meal just like Mary had instructed me to have.

I was feeling numb and disorientated at the dinner. I walked around and talked to everyone, thanking them for coming. I remember Patty, coming and taking me by the arm after a little while and walking me up to the food and helping me get a plate and having me sit with her, John, Kendy, and Mike. Even with my closest friends there with me, I remember feeling abandoned. Some of the guests were talking about Mary and sharing stories, while others were talking about their lives and catching up with each other.

After the service and the meal, Tom, Sarah and I went home to what seemed like a tomb. We had buried Mary next to my dad in our family plot in a rural cemetery not too far from the farm that my great-great-grandfather had once owned and is still owned by my Mom. The three of us talked about the funeral and the service and Mommy and Papa being together.

In some ways, I felt alienated. I felt cut off from the world. That fall what began as a nightmare had now become a full-blown horror movie. I was surprised in many ways by my reaction to some things. Some of my frustration and anger started going away.

Something new started to sink in, something that Mary had told me and explained to me over the last several months before her death and even in our last conversation before she went to the hospital that final time. She had told me that I needed to find someone so that I wouldn't be alone and that would be a good mother to Tom and Sarah, especially Sarah. I was single now and there were things to do.

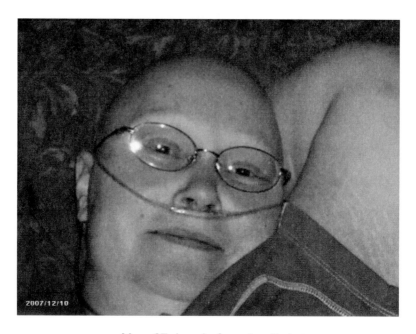

Mary 27 days before she died.

CHAPTER FIFTEEN

<u>Dating!</u>

I still remember very clearly the last good talk that I had with Mary at our house before she went in the hospital. We were sitting in the living room. She was in one reclining chair, and I was in the other. They were facing each other, and she brought up the fact that she was going to die soon.

She told me, "Go find someone." She said, "When I'm gone, you need to go be with a woman who makes you happy. I see how hard it is on you losing your dad."

And then we talked and she asked me my ideas. I told her that during the last several years I had been mourning her death even before she died. We had talked on and off about what the shrink had told me, and I reiterated that, as well as that I thought I would probably heal fairly quick once she was gone, once I didn't have this daily stress of watching her go downhill. She gave me her blessing to go get remarried.

We talked about the type of woman I should find. Mary wanted her to be a good mother and someone who loved me. She said I deserved that. She apologized for not being a better wife. She apologized for being sick. She apologized for not being able to give me more sex. We chuckled at that. When does a man or husband ever get all the sex he wants.

I tried to comfort her by saying that she didn't need to apologize for being sick, that she didn't go out and get cancer on purpose. I reassuringly stressed that she had been a great wife, but that she actually should be sorry for not giving me more sex, and then we laughed again. I guess guys don't change.

So with that in mind, somehow I had a mission, because Mary had emphasized that Tom and Sarah, especially Sarah, needed a mother. We frankly discussed my ability to raise Tom competently. He was already a freshman in college, so not a lot more raising was needed.

Sarah, however, was 12 when we had our conversation. She hadn't started her periods, and I knew that raising a daughter without a mom would be a chore. Mary told me to call her sister when Sarah started menstruating, which she did a week after we buried Mary.

After Mary passed away and we properly buried her, I completed all the estate issues, organized the insurance papers, filed for her retirement from the State - all the things one has to do when a loved one passes away.

And then I thought, "I need to do what Mary told me to," but I tried to put it off a little bit. I just wasn't up to dating, much less finding another wife. It wasn't that I couldn't move on. I just needed a breather. I knew that Mary was dead, which in fact she was, but she was dead to me, also.

Many people with a spouse who dies have trouble letting go, have trouble moving on. That truly wasn't my problem. I was concentrating on the chores at hand, taking care of the kids, taking care of the house, but in the back of my mind about a month after Mary passed, I started thinking about what she had told me, to go find someone.

I had gotten offers before she died, offers from people telling me that when I was single they would fix me up. Friends, neighbors, co-workers, former co-workers, and sometimes that sort of scared me. I didn't really want to be involved with someone with strings to anyone I knew. I was afraid that if the relationship didn't go anywhere I would lose a friend. A classic example of that was the last week Mary was alive.

My Tae Kwon Do instructor, Grand Master Kim, was telling me about his sister. Master Kim and I had known each other since 1987 when I started Tae Kwon Do, and I considered him a very good, dear, and close friend and I still do. He shared his view that men needed to have a wife, that they were much weaker and needed someone to take care of them. I didn't argue that point. He described his sister in Korea and showed me a picture of a very attractive Korean woman. He mentioned that her husband had died several years before from lung cancer, and that she was thinking about coming over to visit him and his family the following summer, in five or six months. He wanted to introduce us to each other. I was polite and thought to myself, "Yeah, she's very attractive. Mary's not dead yet."

I felt awkward, but I knew that Master Kim meant well.

One thing about me that I have always tried to focus on and determine were the person's intentions. I could take an insult or I could take something that was strange or uncomfortable as long as I knew the person meant it well. For me, it was much more of an attitude than an action, and I knew Master Kim meant well. However, as I thought about his offer, I couldn't help but think that if I were to meet his sister, a potentially unsuccessful relationship with her could damage my friendship with Master Kim. I also couldn't help thinking that it was a no-win situation. If I took Master Kim's sister out and I tried to hook up, he'd beat the shit out of me. If I took her out and she wanted me to hook up and I didn't, he'd beat the shit out of me.

So with this in my mind, I thought I needed to start dating. I needed to find somebody myself. I didn't want somebody to fix me up or to find someone for me.

Looking back I think this was a wrong perception on my part. My friends knew me. My friends knew what I wanted. My friends had my best interests at heart. But being the stubborn and independent only child that I had been my whole life, I thought I could do this better on my own, and I was wrong.

I remember Mary listing my good points and bad points in that last conversation. She even suggested a few women who might be good prospects, which creeped me out. She also mentioned several of our friends that had good qualities and told me to find someone like them. She listed my good points as being loyal, faithful, and honest. She also felt that I was a good dad and supportive husband. But she felt honesty and trust were the biggest things that I had going for me.

In 23 years of marriage, I had only told Mary one big lie and that was when I was buying my second male Rottweiler, Nico, from Germany. He was a show dog more than a working dog. He had a great pedigree and turned out to be a wonderful Rottweiler. Nico was more expensive than I really could afford and so, again, I went to my mom and could only get so much money from her - $10,000. The problem was I lied to everyone. Nico was actually $12,500 with the shipping. So I took another loan against a credit card to get the $2,500 that I was short, and I purchased Nico.

I knew I would do well with Nico. He was the Junior National Champion of Germany, a title that they called Bundesjugendsieger. He was a beautiful dog with a great pedigree. He just wasn't a good enough Schutzhund, the Police dog training, for the Germans to keep him in Germany.

When Nico arrived at the airport, I loaded the crate with him in it into my vehicle and drove home. When I pulled in the driveway and tried to take Nico out of the crate to take him in the house, Nico had other ideas. He didn't want to go with me, because he didn't know me. He bolted out of his crate and started running. I was chasing him, and as we went by the window where Mary was standing, she thought, "Why is Mike chasing that dog?"

About 45 minutes later, I came home dogless. Nico had run away and I didn't know where he was. As I was chasing Nico I had encountered my friend, Kendy, who saw me running down the street after this large Rottweiler. She drove her car along side of me and asked what was wrong. I told her, so she drove back to the house and told Mary. Kendy also called some other friends and so did Mary.

I phoned my dad for help, and we started looking for the dog. Night fell, during which time it's pretty hard to find a black dog. When I called the police to make a report and asked them not to shoot a large stray Rottweiler, I told the responding officer how much the dog had cost. Mary and some others heard me, and as they say, "The fat was in the fire," or "The feces hit the oscillator."

That was my one lie to Mary that I got caught in, and I was in trouble. I never lied again, at least about anything big. I guess as a guy and as a husband we always tell our significant other, "Those shoes look wonderful," or "That dress looks fine," when we really don't care, but I guess that's life.

So with that in mind, I also remembered what Mary told me that my bad points were. I was stubborn, I was a poor housekeeper, I was a bad cook, and I held a grudge. So I thought I needed to work on these things if I was going to start dating.

So, knowing my strengths and weaknesses, at least what Mary had told me, and armed with the mission that Mary had given me to go find somebody so I wouldn't be alone and to have a good mother for Tom and Sarah, especially Sarah, I thought about dating and thought I'd better start.

I now was aware at the time that some of my friends thought that I had moved too soon and started dating too quickly, and I truly don't think that was the issue. The Mary that died, in some ways, was not the Mary I had fallen in love with. The cancer had transformed her personality. Mary's role had changed in my life. She had gone from being my lover to being more of a best friend, not that I didn't love Mary, not that I didn't find the idea or the thought of the Mary that I'd married sexy and attractive and desirable. I did. But the last six years that Mary and I were together, our relationship lacked a lot of intimacy and sex.

The last three years that we were married we had no sex. Mary could not do it. The chemo had ravaged her body too much. The chemo was destroying her, and there weren't very many lulls in between the rounds of chemo that allowed us to be intimate. So I truly was ready to move on, and I think that that's true even now looking back.

I started hanging out spending time with some single friends who were females, just really as friends, just hanging out, getting used to talking to women again, maybe flirting a little bit, I don't know. My mental checklist was in high gear, and a couple of the friends just reminded me too much of Mary. Not in physical characteristics or in personality, but they had been our friends, and it just wasn't comfortable.

I talked to another friend, Wayne, who could be described as a little bit of a player. For years he intermittently had placed online ads for dating. In fact, one time when Mary was sick and we were bored, we messed with one of his online ads and had a good joke. Wayne was a good-natured type of guy and he still is, and he laughed. He told me he was going to get even with me sometime and never did.

I ended up calling Wayne and asking him, "How do you do this online dating?"

He had me come over to his house. He taught me how to plug in numbers, facts and figures into the computer and the dating website would show me a list of eligible women that met my criteria.

Wayne was only a year younger than I, 46. When he helped me set up my dating listing, he somehow set it up for women between 18 and 30, and I was flabbergasted. I couldn't help but laugh. Some of the pictures were quite attractive, but they made me feel like a dirty old man. I asked Wayne, "Why would I want to date someone that much younger than me?"

Wayne pointed at the pictures and said, "Man, they're all hot and they need somebody to take them out and treat them nice. Give them a nice dinner and show them a good time."

As we joked and laughed, I said, "But what do we talk about?"

So I pushed him aside, sat down and plugged in my own numbers. I selected women in the age range from 35-50. I also requested at least some college and, preferably, a Bachelor's Degree in the education category. I wanted someone who would be my equal, someone who would be a partner or a potential partner.

Wayne protested, laughed and said, "You don't want that, you want this. You don't want them as smart as you, you want them dumber. You don't want them to be as successful, you want them to be less successful."

Perhaps that strategy worked for Wayne and a lot of men, because I know a lot of men who seem to want women who are beneath them so they can feel empowered. But that wasn't what I wanted. I wanted to find somebody who could be an equal partner with whom I could talk, with whom I could be friends.

214

So Wayne and I went back and forth but, in the end, he succeeded in helping me set up my first online dating ad. When we finished, I thanked him and went home, where I continued to work on my ad. I called him a couple of times with questions and we had some good laughs.

Finally I settled on this ad that said, "Gentleman available to active women."

I listed that I was a widower with two kids. My physical characteristics were, "6'4", fairly athletic, Christian Protestant, didn't smoke, social drinker." For fun I listed that I worked out and did Tae Kwon Do. I stated that my job was teaching junior high and high school special needs students, that I was Methodist, had a strong belief in God and tried to lead a Christian lifestyle as an example to my children. In the category of "education", I stated that I held a Bachelor's Degree and was working on my Master's. I listed my favorite foods as steak and pizza, but no goulash. I'd come to find out that some women think goulash is funny. That was what my grandma made me, but I didn't list it.

I also needed to write a little blurb about myself. I wasn't sure what to write, so I wrote something fairly general/off the top of my head and called Wayne after I was done. As I was reading it to

Wayne, he was rolling on the floor laughing. I felt fairly stupid, but I thought it accurately described me.

I wrote, "I'm a nice guy who's just looking for a friend and thought I might find one in cyberspace. I'm athletic and fit. I like to work out doing cardio workouts and martial arts. I work full-time as a high school teacher. I'm also going part-time to college to get my Master's. I believe in God. I go to church regularly, and I still believe in chivalry. I'm a widower who lost his wife after a very long illness. I can't promise the moon, but I can promise to be a gentleman. I would like to find a nice woman who has similar interests and would like to be fairly active and enjoys family and kids. I'm very involved in my children's lives. If you would like to find one of the few nice guys that's not a player, send me an email."

Wayne laughed and he laughed and he told me I'd never find anyone. He said that was ridiculous.

I actually found a couple. Two different women responded fairly quickly. I had one date with one and two dates with another one. I could soon easily tell that they weren't what I wanted.

One thing I had discovered that was unlike from dating in my 20s to dating in my 40s, was that I knew what I wanted. It was a lot different than when I had dated in college. Before I met Mary, I went

216

out several times to figure things out, to see if I liked the other person. Now, I could more easily read if I had similar interests with a woman, and all I had to do was see if we clicked when we met.

I didn't click with either one of them, and then the third one came along.

It was sort of strange. I found an email from the dating site and it just said, "We seem to have a lot in common and I'd love to hear more. Hope you're having a great weekend and hope to hear from you."

I thought well, it was an attractive picture of her and considering the way the website worked, I think that she realized that I had already looked at her profile. But I didn't initially choose her because the wording in her profile was unrealistic, sounding almost too good to be true, which it was. I ended up emailing her back and that's a story for our next chapter.

CHAPTER SIXTEEN

My Mulligan.

In the sport of golf, a mulligan is something like a redo. A player can redo his shot either because of it simply being a bad shot or due to other circumstances.

So I was single again. I realized that Mary probably knew better than I, that I shouldn't be alone. Sarah and Tom should have a mom, so I started dating. I wanted to date partly for my own personal reasons and partly because of Tom and Sarah, but I wasn't sure what I wanted. Did I want somebody like Mary or would that be too painful? Would that be hard to remember similarities or did I want somebody different? I wasn't sure. And then I was presented an opportunity, my Mulligan.

We went out for the first time three months after Mary died. We talked a lot. It was companionship, emails, texting, phone calls, and I enjoyed it. I thought it was what I needed. Within two and a half months we started getting a little more serious. We still talked a lot through texts and on the phone and amazingly, seven months after Mary died, and four months after meeting Mulligan, I became engaged.

Three months after that we bought a house together in both our names, but I made the down payment. A month after that I bought furniture for the new house, including living room, kitchen, and bedroom suites. Fifteen months after meeting her, I got married. I paid for the honeymoon, most of the wedding, and then a family vacation fairly soon after that. Fourteen months later I told her that I wanted a divorce.

This marriage wasn't what I wanted. This wasn't what I needed. This wasn't working out the way I had expected.

I tried counseling with Mulligan and that didn't work and so, on November 2, 2010, Election Day, I actually voted twice that day, once for elected officials and once for my life. I moved out. I made plans like the experts recommend, like they tell women. A few months before that I realized things weren't going well, and as counseling was going to start, I made a plan. I talked to my mother, moved and I removed most of my belongings, including all of my family heirlooms, out of the house.

The first warning sign should have been that when we were dating things didn't go as expected, plans changed at the last minute, and we could really never stay at my house. That was Mary's house.

The presence of Mary was there, and the presence of Mary seemed to disturb Mulligan.

In retrospect, if Mulligan had had the best intentions when she was dating a widower, the memory of the deceased spouse should not be a disturbance. But I didn't see it at the time, and that was my fault. There were other warning signs that I failed to notice. My beast saw them, but I had locked him away and did not listen to him.

My beast was angry and frustrated, and I didn't have the energy to deal with him after Mary died. It was easier to put a leash and a muzzle on him and lock him away. So I didn't listen to the little voice inside of me.

But being uncomfortable with a deceased spouse, Mulligan should have asked herself if she should even be with that person – me!

Being uncomfortable with a deceased spouse is strange to me. I think if I were dating someone who was a widow, the deceased spouse wouldn't bother me. I would be very comfortable with the fact that they have an angel watching over them. I also think if I were uncomfortable with a deceased spouse, I would expect the widow to ask herself, "Is there a problem here? Hello!"

I think part of my problem was, and I blame myself for this, that I seemed to expect and I do expect from any future spouse what I expected from Mary. I don't expect her to be the boss, and I don't plan to be the boss. Some of the things that Mary would never have done, I wouldn't expect either. I wouldn't have expected Mary to quit her job within six months of us getting married without first telling me. I wouldn't have expected Mary to take money from my checking account and forge my name on a check without telling me. Mary had her own separate checking account from money that she'd earned when she was younger, from money that she'd gotten from the sale of her farm goods, and in 23 years and 2 days of marriage, I never took any money out of her account. I never signed her name to anything without her permission.

I also wouldn't have expected Mary to spend large sums of money on the kids without telling me. There were times that Mary did things that I didn't agree with, but we had talked about them. As well, there were times she just said, "I'm going to do this, but I'm telling you." There were also times I did similarly with her. When Mary married me, she left the past behind. I know she had boyfriends before me, as I'd had girlfriends before her, but when we got married, we felt that we moved forward - together. I can also guarantee that I

221

never would have expected or tolerated Mary emailing an old boyfriend's family when she'd promised me she wouldn't.

One thing that I learned in 23 years of marriage to Mary was that we would tell the other one the truth. My one exception was when I bought Nico. I lied about the price by about $2,500, and that was a big deal. But I learned that one never lies to one's spouse.

So, one of the main things, if not the main thing, as I look to the future, as I look for my hope on the horizon, when I try to find that fairytale that I once had with Mary, is that I will not tolerate any future wife not telling me the truth, not being honest with me, even on little things, like where she went with friends or what restaurant she ate in, or the price she would spend on the kids' cell phones.

Before my Mulligan round, I should've listened to my friends, especially my female friends. Somehow I think my female friends have a pretty good intuition. My good friend, Denise, who was our housekeeper for over 10 years, who we used to call our Hazel and would call herself our Hazel, gave me some great advice but I didn't listen. Does Mulligan do what she says she will? Does she break dates and or plans? If she doesn't keep her word to you now, she won't if and when you would get married. Mulligan broke her word and plans all the time when we were dating.

I then did something that I'm very ashamed of. After I bought my house with Mulligan, she mentioned something that I regret listening to and that was Denise's salary was too high. Mulligan also offered to help clean my old house in order to save that money. This was especially tempting, considering that I would have to support two mortgages for a short time until I sold my house. The funny thing was no one ever came to my house to help. Apparently, the ghost of Mary scared her away.

Another very good and dear friend, Patty, my human Rottweiler, also gave me some advice that I didn't listen to. Sign a prenuptial agreement that says who will pay for what, make a list that includes the children's bills.

My dear friend, Kendy, who was also Patty's and my sister from another mother, said that I needed to use Mary as a measuring stick on how a new woman in my life treated both me and my kids.

My friend Mike, who's like a brother to me, is married to a sweet woman named Carrie. Carrie just recently told me that, after her and Mike went out to dinner one night with me and my Mulligan, she went home and cried, because Mulligan wasn't my type of woman and I didn't see it. She was sad for me. She didn't know what to say. She didn't know how to tell me that she had these feelings.

Mary's friends were very cold. I don't think they knew how to react with me moving on. But I should have listened, I should have felt the cold, and I should've come in out of the blizzard into the warmth of their hearts and their good intentions. Most of my friends and even my guy friends have told me that it was going to be hard to find someone similar to Mary, someone who loved me for me myself, my personality, someone who didn't love me for my material things. And I realize that's true.

Part of the problem was that I had locked up my beast. I wasn't balanced. I wouldn't listen to him. I was frustrated and tired and I didn't want to have any anger or negative feelings so soon after I buried Mary. I didn't listen to him until several months after I was married again.

I was at Tae Kwon Do sparring with somebody who was around 30 years old. He was new to Tae Kwon Do, but he was athletic and in good shape, and I was trying to teach him during a sparring lesson. I don't even know his name. He wouldn't listen and he kept coming after me with a strong attack, with some good moves, and it pissed me off. He kept trying to kick my knees to take me down. It didn't happen. I blocked and I moved out of the way and I tried to explain. And after four or five times, my beast broke his chains and came roaring back into my consciousness. I punched and kicked and sparred at a level that one would expect a Tae Kwon Do Master to be.

After I executed a few more hits and kicks, I tried to explain again to this man what he was expected to do and not to do, and trying to take someone out at the knees who's attempting to help him learn is not appropriate. I don't know why this new student was so intent on kicking my knees, but it just infuriated me. He wouldn't listen, he wouldn't change. After a few more exchanges on my part - punches to the face, kicks to the stomach, everything that was legal above the belt, he dove at me. I caught him, I blocked him, I parried his attack, and he ended up in a headlock. For a few moments, a split second maybe, the beast inside of me roared.

Everything flashed through my mind that I had been taught for years and years and was expected to use in self-defense when I worked in prison. There were several ways I could snap his neck, and my beast begged to do it. The anger inside me flared up and I was mad. All the rage and frustration that I'd had, that I was living, surged through me. Should I just sit down with his head in my arm? Should I roll and twist to one side or the other? But within that fraction of a second, in those few moments, my gentle side won out. I let him go and walked away.

But I questioned myself. Why was I so angry and what was I so frustrated about? And then it dawned on me that things were not what I had planned them to be, and that this was truly a Mulligan round. I needed a do-over. I needed to start over. I wanted to have peace and happiness. I was tired. I didn't want to worry. I didn't want any stress. I wanted my fairytale life back. And I realized that this fairytale had turned out to be a Grimm fairytale. I reflected on what I wanted and why I wanted to do it. Expectations were placed on me by Mulligan that I didn't want and I didn't expect. We had talked before we even became engaged and her three children from her two previous marriages where going to stay being her responsibility and had now become mine. However, as time went on she expected me to take care of their financial needs. She took one of her ex-husbands back to court for him to pay more for his children's college bills and he wanted to bring my financial records into court. This was not what I expected when I became engaged.

When I had talked to Mary before she passed, we always planned for when she was gone and for when I could find someone else with whom to continue my fairytale. My plans were, and I had

226

always said this, that I would take care of my choices and I would take care of my children. I'd always said that I wouldn't take care of choices that I did not make. I'd always said that I would not pay for decisions that I was not able to participate in. I realized that I had made a Mulligan. I started thinking in a more balanced manner now that my beast was with me again. My gentle side and my consciousness embraced the beast as an old friend and were glad that he was back.

One of the things that I've learned in Tae Kwon Do is that sparring must be balanced. In many ways, life is like a sparring match. It must be balanced. If there is no balance, then there is no happiness. If there is no balance, there's no peace.

Sarah and Tom 2007.

CHAPTER SEVENTEEN

Single Again.

I moved to Mom's house with Sarah on November 2, 2010, Election Day. My son, Tom, helped. He was at the house when Sarah and I moved out. He helped us load our clothes, not only in the bags that we were putting them in, but he also helped load them into the vehicles. I had two SUVs that we had to take. I called what I did an inmate move. We took large garbage bags and loaded them with clothes. I already had as much moved as I could, including some of my storage boxes and some of my family keepsakes. I planned this ahead of time with my mom. I was disappointed. I was disappointed that counseling didn't work. I was disappointed in the situation, but I knew that I had to plan for the worst, to hope for the best but plan for the worst.

Tom drove one SUV and I drove the other. From start to finish, it only took between 30-40 minutes for Sarah and I to get everything ready to go. I had it planned with her, if and when I made the decision, this is what we had to do. Making the decision was hard. There were things I couldn't tolerate and couldn't change. What were priorities once in my life had to be again. Those priorities were God and my kids. I don't blame anybody except myself, but I felt as if God was slipping away from me, and I realized the kids only had me for everything: support, money, caring. I was their mother and their father.

I had thought for some time that children of divorced parents had Christmas with one parent and then would have to get up and go to the other parent's house. They had two Christmases. My children had two Christmases. They have the Christmas with me. The other Christmas they have is also with me, but it's at the cemetery at the grave of my father and Mary, paying our respects, thinking of things that could've been but never will.

I thought of the saying, "Do not pity the dead. Pity the living." When we were at the cemetery on Christmas day, I pitied Tom and Sarah, who only had me, and I felt as if I were letting them down. I also had to make decisions based on protecting myself and the promises I made to Mary. Step kids would never come before Tom and Sarah. I'm their only parent. I'm their only-only.

Being single again didn't scare me. I had no fear about being alone this time. After a bad or wrong relationship, I felt relief when I left the Mulligan.

I was disheartened and embarrassed, too. When I talked to my lawyer, Ronnie, about the divorce and filling out the papers, I

229

expressed my shame and embarrassment to him. I never in my life thought I'd ever be divorced. But Ronnie was great. He'd known my dad for years and liked him. They were friends. He gave me advice like my father would have, and for that I'll always be grateful. It's amazing, as I look back on this journey of mine, this battle, this war with breast cancer that I'd been fighting and all the people who have been kind and have opened their hearts and their feelings and even their homes to me. It touches me and gives me hope for the future.

But I still have the hope of finding the right one. I still have faith that God will put me in the right relationship. So, being single again didn't bother me. In considering what to do for the future, I remembered the phrase, "Insanity is doing the same thing over and over again but expecting different results." So this time as a single man and as a single parent, I will do this differently. I will let friends introduce me to women they think would be my type. I'm not going to avoid that like I did the first time. My friends know women who have the positive qualities that I expect, and I realize that's the type of woman I'm attracted to.

I was going to try online dating again along with allowing my friends to introduce me to people. After the divorce papers had been sent but were not final yet, I was sitting one night in my living room playing with my computer. I was setting up my profile on one of the online sites. My friend, Kendy, called to check in with me and asked what I was doing and how I was doing, and we talked for a little bit about a variety of topics and about the kids.

Then she said, "Well, what are you doing right now?"

I told her.

She screamed, "No!"

I almost dropped the phone. I asked her what she was telling me "no" about?

She said that she had someone for me that she wanted me to meet, but I said wouldn't date until my divorce was final. She agreed.

But she said, "Stop working on that profile. I have someone for you."

Kendy described the qualities of this woman. I liked what I heard. But I reminded Kendy that I didn't like surprises. She told me she wouldn't surprise me, but I wasn't sure if I believed her.

When the divorce was final, I asked Kendy for the woman's phone number, and I called her. We talked and joked and laughed about blind dates and how everybody would typically ask what other person's favorite color was and so forth…really inane things!

The day before the official blind date occurred, I, surprisingly, ended up going to lunch with what would turn out to be a new hope.

The next day we had our official blind date with Kendy, her husband, Glen, and my friends John and Patty. It renewed my hope to have my friends so concerned about me, to want me to be happy, to find somebody that would match with me.

My desire is to find someone that has the specific qualities, values and ethics I'm searching for. I'm never going to give up hope. I realize I need somebody who's loyal, honest and trustworthy, someone who has my back, someone who is fiscally or financially responsible, someone who goes to church fairly regularly, and someone who has kids who have been raised similarly as my own have, have been raised with similar values as my own have - children that are respectful, polite, and not self-centered. I'm someone who believes in romance and has hope to find it. The bottom line is that I want someone who believes the same way as I do.

I think I can find a hope who has all of these qualities. My hope should make me feel very comfortable and relaxed, something that I haven't felt for a long, long time. As I was writing this book and talking about different things, I realized that it's been a long time since I've felt the way I do. I want to have fun with just my hope at times, but I also need to have someone who I can include as an intimate part of my life, who is able to have fun with me and my friends. I realize now what I didn't realize before, that having friends in common is good, and it's what I want, because when one has friends in common, we both can enjoy the same group of people.

I've learned a lot from the first time I was single. I don't know what's going to happen with this new Hope, as I write this, but I do know this, since I started this book, the light, the little flicker at the end of the tunnel of hope is brighter now. It's still a ways off. Something can come along and dim that light, one never knows. But I have hope and faith and they go together, and true hope can never die.

I'll always have hope as I look for the right woman to invite into my life and into the lives of my children. Someone I can love, someone I can trust and feel secure with. Someone whose beauty I can marvel at for all the days I have left, because I have learned that beauty is in the eye of the beholder, and beauty radiates from the inside out.

Most women don't seem to think men think that way. I, however, think we do, deep down inside. Other men may not admit it, but I do. I believe my faith will get me my new hope someday, whether it's this hope or the next hope on the horizon.

Patty, Kendy, and me in 2010. Two of the most protective and loyal friends I could ever have.

CHAPTER EIGHTEEN

My Faith.

I was baptized and confirmed a Methodist, and the Methodist faith, from my interpretation and experience, seems to embrace the doctrine of putting faith and love into action, and trusting God as a source and destiny of our lives. My parents were Methodist. As Methodists, we also believe in reading the Bible and interpreting it through our own experiences and being saved through the blood of Jesus Christ. I truly believe that. I read the Bible and I interpret it based on my experiences, about which I am now writing.

Some of my experiences, though, I haven't touched on. My mom's mother, Grandma Jones, was evangelical, nor did she go to one church in particular, but that's how I would describe her philosophical beliefs as being evangelical. She had a sister named El, who was my great-aunt, but I would call her Aunt El. She claimed to have the gift of prophecy. When I was 15, she told my grandma something about me, about how I would be tough and how God was with me. She quoted a Bible scripture from Joshua about the old story of Gideon. In a lot of ways, I am like Gideon. I have periods of doubt as did he, and I keep asking God to prove something to me. But something else about the story of Gideon seems to relate to me, and that is that Gideon never gave up, even when faced with overwhelming odds, and it seems like I haven't either.

I believe in God and Jesus and the Holy Spirit, and I believe that some people do have the gift of prophecy, that the Holy Spirit gives them that. From my interpretations of the Bible, not everyone who has the Holy Spirit in him or her has the gift of prophecy. I feel that I have the Holy Spirit in me and that somehow it's guiding me. It's guiding me to do what God wants me to do. My faith also embraces things from other religions, however, one ongoing experience that I've had has been very interesting. I've had dreams throughout my life, and sometimes they come true. One dream in particular stands out. It was in the month of May before my dad died the following August. I dreamed that my mom was standing in the doorway to my bedroom, that somehow I was looking at this scene from the foot of my bed, and my mom uttered the words, "I can't believe that Don is gone."

It was as simple and as brief as that and then I woke up. I was petrified. Somehow I knew that dream was real. It was almost as if Death himself had put his cold hands on my shoulders and shook me awake.

I woke up Mary in a panicked state and told her about the dream. I bolted upright, stood at the foot of the bed as I had been in

236

the dream, and Mary had to talk me out of calling my dad and waking him up in the middle of the night. I so intensely wanted to make sure he was all right. Mary assured me it was just a dream, that he was fine and that somehow, subconsciously, I was just worrying about him getting older. It wasn't until after my dad had died and Mary was in the hospital, August 22, 2007, the day after my father had died, that that dream became reality.

The day after my father had passed I couldn't sleep very well. I had put the pillows at the foot of the bed so that my head now faced the door. My mom was staying at the house. The lights were the same as my dream. The only light on in the hallway was the bathroom light that shined out the door. It was exactly as my dream had predicted. I woke up with a start to see my mom standing in the door, and she uttered the very same words, "I can't believe that Don is gone."

Looking back I believe that the Holy Spirit wanted to prepare me for what was coming.

Over the years, I've experienced what might be called strong intuitive or gut feelings, thoughts that would pop into my head that might be termed as predictive of things to come, and I still am not sure where they come from. I don't want to sound arrogant or boastful, but

I do want to sound sincere. There were intermittent times that I had these foreshadowings.

One that immediately comes to mind is when I was in college before I'd even met Mary. I was dating a girl by the same name. Her mother had died of breast cancer and, for some reason, we had a date. On that date, Mary expressed concern and worry that she would die from breast cancer. I remember, after I dropped her off at home and was driving back to my house, I said a prayer to God not to let Mary have breast cancer and die like her mother. A little thought popped into my head that God would honor that prayer, that request, but that I would one day marry a woman and she would die of breast cancer. I put the thought out of my mind and pooh-poohed it. It bothered me though and, from time to time when I would hear the words "breast cancer", I would think about it. It wasn't until Mary was diagnosed with breast cancer that the fear, the little cold feeling that had crept in when I'd had that thought started to grow then.

I do have faith in God. I do believe that God has a purpose for all of us. I believe that my purpose is to be an example of keeping my faith. I didn't know that or feel that until I really started this book, but I believe it now. I used to be like the prodigal son's brother. I'd always tried to follow God's laws and rules. I always tried to be good,

238

but somehow, like the prodigal son's brother who never left, I was hard-hearted and judgmental. Through this journey of life, which has included my war with cancer, I've learned that I can't judge others, and my heart has softened.

I learned about being saved when I was five. I was always a Christian. I was raised in a Christian household. Some of my earliest memories were of going to my local Methodist Church. I had the normal struggles growing up, but I still remember when I was five of hearing some people talk about being saved. I asked my mom and dad, "What does that mean? What are they saved from?" Somehow in my little kid's mind, I was thinking about being saved from a dog that was chasing me.

My father explained to me that "being saved" was a belief that Jesus was God's Son and He had died on the cross to save everyone and that because of Christ's selfless act, we would all be saved and get to go to Heaven when we died. In order to attain heaven, we just had to believe that Jesus was the Son of God and He had died on the cross for us.

I remember thinking that that was about the most obvious thing to me. I couldn't help but chuckle when I watched the *Forrest*

Gump movie years later and people talked about finding God and finding Jesus, and Forrest Gump said, "I didn't know He was lost."

I didn't go to church every Sunday as an adult. I probably went once every three or four months. I went to Sunday School regularly as a child, but as an adult who worked and had responsibilities, I seemed to never have time to go every Sunday. I regret that now, but I did read the Bible daily through most of high school and college and as an adult. When Dad died, I realized how lost I truly was, and I started going just about every Sunday. I had stopped attending church when I was with Mulligan, and that bothered me. I didn't feel the presence of God at that time in my life like I did before or I do now.

I've now returned to attending church every Sunday. Actually, I go to a Bible Study on Sunday mornings, which I call Sunday School. I feel much closer to God. I feel His presence in my life every day. That presence strengthens me in my ongoing war against breast cancer, which I continue to fight even though Mary is gone. It heals the scars. It gives me strength to go on. But I also feel that my faith gives me other gifts.

There is a term some theologians have talked about called beaming. Beaming is when a Christian soul goes to heaven and

240

wants to communicate for some reason with a loved one back on earth. My Grandma Stalter has done that with me three times as I previously mentioned, my Dad twice, and Mary three times.

My dad came back about six weeks after he passed and told me he was okay. He was sitting in a chair next to my bed. I asked him how he was, and he said fine.

I replied, "No, I mean about your heart attack."

He said he was okay. And I woke up.

The second time that I dreamed of my father, he was in church and I wasn't, and he was waving at me. Somehow I think he knew that I needed to come back to God, to find my faith, and to keep it strong.

Mary had come to me three times after she died. I was disappointed in some ways before that I'd never gotten to say goodbye to the healthy Mary, to the one I'd fallen in love with, to the one of my youth. So one night Mary appeared to me, as the young Mary looked before she got cancer, and she told me goodbye. We talked for a little bit. She told me to remember all she had said to me, what she had instructed me to do before she died and to take care of Tom and Sarah.

When I was thinking about beginning to date again and was looking for someone to share my life with, I woke up from a dream that Mary, the sick Mary, the Uncle Fester Mary, was in my bedroom, our old bedroom, cleaning. I asked, "What are you doing? You're dead, you came back to clean our bedroom?"

She told me yes, she was and that I certainly wouldn't get a good wife with a messy house.

Then I woke up.

I interpreted that dream to mean that she was giving me her blessing, as she had in life, to move on, to find someone and to be happy, as she had told me to that last week she was home.

I never dreamed about Mary during my second marriage. She never came to me. It wasn't until I'd moved out and right before the divorce was final that she appeared in my dreams again.

She looked like an angel. She was perfect. It wasn't the Mary of my youth. It wasn't the Mary that I'd ever known. But it was Mary. Gone were all the scars. Her hair and her face looked as if she was in her 40s like she should be, but she was perfect. I could tell through the shape of her clothes that she had both breasts, no swollen arms, no scars. I asked her what she was doing, and she told

242

me she was just checking in on me to make sure that I was all right. And then I woke up.

That's given me some comfort knowing that Mary's watching over me. I believe in these dreams. Some people reading this may think I'm crazy, or they were just dreams like all dreams. I can't explain it, I can't justify it. I only have my faith to go on, but I truly believe in what the theologians say that this was a beaming from the three most important people in my life.

Sarah also had one of these experiences right after Mary died. She was so inconsolable that I didn't know what to do. Sarah had dreamed that she woke up and could smell Mary's cooking. The last few years before Mary died, she couldn't do much work around the house, but she'd tinker in the kitchen, making baked goods and desserts. It would fill the whole house with the smell of whatever she was making. Sarah described her dream as waking up and coming downstairs from her bedroom and smelling Mommy cooking. She walked in the kitchen, and there, in her regular spot, sat Mary. Sarah told me that she asked, "Mommy, what are you doing here? You're dead."

Mary replied that yes she was dead, but she knew Sarah needed a hug.

The last few months that Mary was alive, Sarah had to be very careful to not bump Mary's stomach, so as Sarah went to give her a very gentle hug, Mary pulled her into a tight embrace and wasn't worried. They talked for a little bit and then my dad, who Sarah called Papa, walked into the kitchen and didn't say a word to Sarah but hugged her. And then Sarah woke up.

I feel very comfortable in my relationship with God. He doesn't give me everything I ask for, but He's always there. Mostly these days, I just ask for strength and, that, He's giving me. Somehow I've always felt that I serve in the role of protector of my friends and family. After leaving Corrections when I was taking some classes to add to my teaching certificate, I took a personality test. It was quite extensive and took a couple hours. In the end, it said my personality was that of a guardian protector, which encompasses only 1% of the population, and explains why I've always felt different when I hear people talk about being one of God's sheep. I realize now that I am part of God's flock. I'm just one of the Rottweiler guard dogs roaming the edges, guarding the sheep.

I realize, too, that God gave me Sarah. I look back on the night that she was conceived. Mary was just meant to conceive and that is the only way I can explain that night. Sarah truly was a

244

blessing. It seems that, as hard as it was to get Sarah conceived, there had to be some purpose in God's plan. When I sat at my dad's grave gripping my knife, just one small twitch from shoving it in, I think Sarah was my last lifeline to not doing it. God moves in mysterious ways as they say, and I feel He has guided my life. I need to realize and do what He wants me to do.

When I first met my blind date, somewhere in one of our early conversations I told her part of my story. She'd known a lot. Kendy had told her. One of the comments she made was she was amazed that I still had faith. I've never lost my faith in God throughout this long war with breast cancer and its aftermath. At times I feel that God is playing or had played a cruel joke on me, because of all of the suffering I've been through.

However, I think of the suffering of Christ and what He went through to save me, and I realize that my suffering is nothing compared to His. So I'm humbled to think that God could be using me to help others, to assist and support other husbands and men to better understand what their wives, girlfriends and even mothers go through and think about as they battle a terminal or potentially terminal illness.

Men are from Mars and women are from Venus. We react differently. Most men don't share their feelings, so maybe that's my job. My faith has also comforted me when I'm down or scared, although I don't get down very often anymore these days. I fear very few things. After what I've been through, after what I've seen, I don't fear much. The things I do fear is the loss of either Tom or Sarah or someone I love and care about, and the people, the friends and family I'm attached to. I try to marvel at this amazing world that God has created for us. I still have Faith that God will guide my path in life and won't burden me with more than I can carry.

Sarah her Freshman year in high school.

CHAPTER 19

Tom and Sarah.

Tom was born February 7, 1989. Mary was diagnosed with cancer, October 1, 1990. Tom was 18 months old when Dr. Hough found the lump. Tom only knew Mary as sick, but she appeared fairly normal and healthy until Tom was in fourth grade. During her first round of chemo and surgeries, Tom became very close to me, as I was the care-giving parent during Mary's first cancer treatment, which lasted until May of 1991. It took a few more months after she was done with chemo in May for Mary to get her strength back.

Tom became a little closer with Mary as time went on, but in May of 1994, Mary became pregnant with Sarah and, again, I became Tom's primary caregiver. Mary seemed to sleep a lot while she was pregnant. It just tired her out. When Sarah was born, Mary really relished in being able to care for Sarah. She loved being given a second chance with a second child. It was a good time in our lives, and things were good for Tom until March of 1999 when the cancer came back.

Looking back, I think that Mary was unusually tired during Sarah's pregnancy, because the cancer was growing in her. Dr. Hough advised us to have Mary's tubes tied after Sarah was born. He couldn't prove it by studies, but he was worried that if Mary should become pregnant again, the pregnancy could weaken the system and allow the cancer to return. He was also worried about the odds of the breast cancer returning. He knew how often breast cancer came back when it started out in women so young.

Right after Sarah was born Mary decided to have her tubes tied. Mary knew Sarah was going to be her last child, and she enjoyed Sarah as much as any mother ever enjoyed a child.

Sarah was born on January 5, 1995. Mary wanted to do everything with her, because I believe that Mary was subconsciously thinking that the cancer could return like Dr. Hough had advised us. It could come back at any time, and she wanted Sarah to know her. She wanted Sarah to realize that she had a mother who loved her and wanted to care for her.

Sarah had just turned four and in March, 1999, we discovered the cancer had come back. Sarah reflected that she never really remembered or knew a mother who wasn't sick.

Tom's friends and classmates were good to Tom during Mary's battle with cancer. The only negative thing that occurred was that the kids would tell Tom that they were sorry, because everyone with cancer dies. When Tom told us that, we tried to reassure him

248

that he would be ok and that I would be there for him and Mary would too as long as she could. Now, when I talk with Tom, he tells me that he knew it was true, and we were just trying to comfort him.

When Mary did pass away during Tom's freshman year in college, his old high school wrestling team came as one big group to Mary's visitation. Tom was truly blessed with a lot of close and caring friends along with a great coach.

Sarah, on the other hand, seemed to have the opposite experience. Sarah was in the seventh grade and had a few friends in school. Many of her classmates made fun of her because of how Mary looked and the fact that Mary was sick with cancer. Sometimes, the kids wouldn't play with Sarah. They'd say things like, "If you play with Sarah, you could catch cancer."

Sarah had a much tougher time with school than Tom did and, in many ways, I think Sarah had a much tougher time overall with everything about Mary's illness. She was younger when the cancer came back. I don't think she understood. She only had this gnawing fear that something was wrong with Mommy.

Tom is more like Mary's family who are stoic and hold in their emotions. Sarah is much more like me. She shows her emotions much more and does not care who sees them when she does.

249

As I was writing this book my friend, Kendy, stopped and wanted to take Sarah and me out to eat. As we were sitting at the restaurant talking, catching up, having a good time, we started discussing the book that I was writing. Sarah started to get watery eyes and then cried a little bit. I looked at Kendy and she returned my glance, because a few days before that, Kendy had told me she didn't really remember seeing Sarah cry other than when Mary died. However, that day at the restaurant, Sarah did cry in front of Kendy. Sarah is much more emotional than Tom ever was. She cries at night when she thinks no one can hear, but I hear. Sometimes, most times I will go to Sarah and talk with her. She tries to be brave and stop when she sees me. I don't know which is better. I think it's probably better to let one's emotions out rather than to bottle them up.

After Mary died though, Tom went through a very angry and almost violent time like I did when she was sick. That lasted for a couple years, and Tom now seems to be getting out of it. Tom described it as just having a very short fuse. He couldn't tolerate "stupid," as he puts it and, when he dealt with stupid people, stupid comments, or stupid things, he became very frustrated and irate.

Tom also moved away from home at the end of his sophomore year to share an apartment with some friends from college. He admits now that he drank quite a bit. His grades fell for a while, and he struggled for about two years, but he's been doing well this last year. His grades are up, his work evaluations are outstanding, and he has been promoted and given a couple of raises. He wants to be in Business Management.

When I moved away from our home town for my second marriage, Sarah excelled at a new high school. She was able to start fresh, with no one having known about Mary, no one having known what Mary looked like or had turned into. Sarah just told people at her new school that her mom had died of cancer and left it at that. Sarah made the cheerleading squad for both football and basketball her freshman year. She was asked to go to the dances and seemed to always have a lot of friends. A typical weekend for her would be having slumber parties at our house and going to slumber parties. Sarah was accepted, and nobody worried about catching cancer from her.

When Sarah and I moved back to Pontiac, when I realized I had made a mulligan, she was a little apprehensive, but she did very well, and she continues to do very well. She went out for the wrestling team, and capably wrestled against the boys, and she had a lot of fun. She has no fear. She also went out for track in the spring and pole vaulted, which I still find quite humorous, because Sarah's only five feet tall. Mary was also short, being only 5 feet 1 inch.

As I write this book, in fact as I'm writing this chapter right now, Sarah is starting her junior year in high school. She's on the cross country team and is planning on wrestling when the cross country season's over and wrestling starts. She dreams of doing well in pole vault this spring. We'll just have to see. She's excited about starting classes in nursing. She's taken a Certified Nursing Assistant's class through the vocational program at the high school. Sarah's dream is to become an oncology nurse and help those suffering with cancer. From her experience with her mother and what Sarah has gone through with that, she also thinks that she can help the families of cancer victims.

Overall, Tom and Sarah have moved on very well and are good kids of whom any father would be extremely proud. There are times I think they've done well despite me. There are times I think that I could've done more, could've been a better parent, could've been more understanding and patient. I guess like life, being a parent is just doing the best I can, and Tom and Sarah know I have. Yet as a parent I have regrets centered on not doing more or simply being better at parenting.

252

Someone recently told me that I must've done something right, since Sarah isn't getting in trouble and using drugs after what she's been through. Tom and Sarah have been through a lot, and they are thriving and moving forward with their lives. Only time will be able to tell if they will continue to do as well in the future as they are doing now.

My Dad, Tom, and I. 2006

CHAPTER 20

Reflections!

Looking back over these past 21 years, I've learned a lot, I've changed a lot. I'm stronger than that 14-year-old boy who argued with his dad over wrestling, or that 30-year-old kid who found out 10 days after his birthday that his wife had cancer. My emotions aren't rock hard like they used to be. My dad's death changed all that. I have trouble holding in emotions and tears at times when something touches me.

One night I stopped by Mike and Carrie's house, my friend who I worked with at the prison and his wife, when I was driving around town feeling lonely. It was about five months after Mary had died. They were outside and saw me, they waved for me to stop, and they were both so kind. We talked for a while and visited and then they invited me to stay and eat supper with them. All through the meal, I was choked up by their kindness. Mike reflected on Mary and how she used to baby and mother him when he was single. I now think they were repaying Mary that night by opening their home and hearts to me.

A tear rolled down my cheek. I apologized for being a pussy. Carrie laughed and said, "You're the toughest pussy I know."

I said I couldn't control my emotions since Dad had died and it bothered me.

Mike asked me why. Without waiting for an answer, he said, "You walked in some of the most dangerous places in the country, some of the meanest, toughest cell houses that there are without protection, no gun, no mace, nothing at all, and how many guys can say that they did that? So who cares if you get choked up after what you've been through?"

I realized he was right. Mike is the brother I never had.

The more I share my story, my feelings, my emotions it seems the stronger I get. I have walked in some of the country's most dangerous halls. I've killed the mother of my children. I really don't have anything left to prove.

One thing that does bother me is that statistically, 70% of the men who are married to terminally ill women will divorce them within two years of finding out that they've been diagnosed as incurable. Women, in one study, are six times as likely to be dumped as men are when they have a serious or terminal illness.

Another study in the United Kingdom said that women are seven times as likely to be dumped as men when one of the spouses has a terminal illness.

These statistics are based on some of the studies by United States doctors. Men are less able to be caregivers. These numbers are staggering and embarrassing.

I remember the first time I learned of the research studies was in the eight years that Mary seemed to be cancer free. I was very mad when I read them. I can understand the data, however, as there were times that I wanted to leave. There were times that I wanted to go hide out in the Unabomber's cabin. However, I didn't.

If I can save one woman or one child the pain of abandonment by an unempathetic husband or a father, then I think this book was worth it.

I have become emotionally, mentally, spiritually and physically stronger than I ever thought I would be over these last 21 years, and I think I'm as strong as my dad wanted me to be all those years ago when he first made me go out for wrestling. I've come to accept my beast as a tool, an asset to be used when needed.

I've told people that it's like watching *Star Wars*. At first, in the first movie, Luke Skywalker is terrified of his dark side, but by the third movie he learns how to use it when he has to fight Darth Vader. Luke learns how to control his dark side. When he beats Darth Vader by using his dark side, he puts it away. Luke learned to control his dark side, as I have mine. I've learned that life is a test between good and evil, God and Satan. I want to think that good has won and I'm one of God's victories.

Mary changed during her battle with breast cancer. She showed everyone who knew her how to die with dignity and compassion. Our friend, Denise, was at our home one day to clean about a month before Mary died, and she was crying over how deteriorated Mary had become. And I still remember Mary holding Denise's hand and telling her it would be all right. Mary was comforting her friend over her own death.

Mary's last words to Tom and Sarah were that she would see them in heaven. She showed us all how to die with dignity, grace and courage.

Sarah was the miracle baby that God gave us so that I wouldn't kill myself when I was standing at Dad's grave. Reflecting back, I see the brilliance of God's plan for me. He knew I would stay to protect my little girl no matter how much pain I was in. I think of all the ways God has blessed me, in so many ways, and even through this experience, this war, life has been a blessing.

Soko, my Rottweiler, was a lifeline that transcends time. His strength and determination inspire me to this day. He was the ultimate wingman. He never left my side. He never failed in his loyalty to me. He never backed down from a challenge, and I remember his attitude and tenacity whenever doubt starts to creep into my mind. At that time, the memory of Soko is there to help push that doubt away.

I've learned to be more understanding and empathetic with other people, not to judge them, because I don't know what they've been through. Who knows, they may have been through more than I. I have an old friend who lost three siblings and his parents in a few short years, and by his own admission, he was an emotional wreck for a time. Then he made God his priority, and now he's a better man, a better husband, and a better father. I think of him and his friendship often, along with the good times we had.

Sooner or later we all will lose our parents and grandparents, and half of us will lose our spouses. It can be hard and it can be devastating, but I've learned and always remember that my parents and grandparents and Mary loved me very much. They gave me a gift that was priceless. They gave me their knowledge. They shared their lives and life stories with me. In my darkest, coldest, loneliest times, those stories and love come back to me. They give me the will and

258

fortitude to get up from the hardest hits that life can give me and have kept me moving forward.

I look back at Mary's last Christmas card and now I see how precious that gift was. She valued me and told me how important I had been in her life. She was trusting me to protect, care for, and nourish her children when she was gone. What more could a woman trust you with than her own children?

In her last words to me, turning to me when the pain was more than she could take, I realize that her dependence on my strength was what helped her. I now feel ashamed of how many times I almost gave up. Never again will I think of giving up. I didn't even realize how much my own wife needed me.

My struggles since Mary died have continued to focus on trying to rebuild my life, and I realize that my friends truly do care about me. There's an old saying that a person is rich if they have one true friend. I realize that I am blessed and richer than I could ever have imagined. I have so many true friends that have helped me on this journey through life, through this war with cancer, and they've always stayed with me. I have mentioned some of them in this book and, as I reflect, their impact on my life is great. I wouldn't be the person I am today without them. They helped keep me going, and some were even told by Mary to watch over me and help me move on after she was gone.

My faith has come through this war with cancer stronger than I ever thought it would and stronger than when the battle started. I have faith that God will give me what I need and sustain my hope that I will have the happy fairytale that I once had and I hope to have again.

I will never give up hope for that partner in life. I will never stop looking until I find just the right woman, even if it takes the rest of my life, even if I don't find her. No matter how old we get, we still have emotional needs and that is to meet someone special and fall in love. Even the Bible tells us that we should find a partner.

I have learned that I can choose the path I walk down, the path of anger with the past, or the path of happiness with the future. I have learned to try new things, like how much fun it is to ride a three wheeled motorcycle, called a Spyder. I have learned of the wisdom to look inside and pray for an answer. Having my hope is believing again, trusting again and looking forward to simple pleasures again.

I don't know where my life will end up, but I still have faith that wherever it does, it will be okay.

If I could make my life into a movie, I would be John Wayne in *Angel and the Badman*, and it would end with me and my Hope riding off—not in the back of a wagon like John Wayne and Gail Russell did, but we would ride off on my Spyder.

Mary taught me how to die. My Hope, is teaching me how to live.

My friend Mike September 2010.